30 STARTLING PROOFS & PROPHECIES

Proving That God Exists

Peter & Paul Lalonde

Prophecy Partners Inc.
P.O. Box 665, Niagara Falls, Ontario L2E 6V5

Unless otherwise noted, all scripture quotations are taken from the King James Bible.

Canadian Cataloguing Publication Data

Lalonde, Peter
301 Startling Proofs and Prophecies: Proving That God Exists

Mass paper ed.
ISBN 0-9680758-1-9
1.God - Proof. 1. Lalonde, Paul, 1961- Title
III. Title: Three hundred and one startling proofs and prophecies.

BT102.L34 1997   231'.042   C96-901058-3

Part 1:
Startling Proofs

Part 2:
Startling Prophecies

To Patti

In the twelve years that we've been married, I've always been amazed at the way the Lord uses you for His kingdom. You usually toil quietly in the background, but Paul and I thought that our readers should know that this book would not have been possible without your dedication and comprehensive research.

Startling Proofs

Introduction

The creation of the universe and the beginning of life on Earth were one time events. How they came about can never be proven by science which requires repeated experimentation and observable empirical evidence. Nonetheless, many believe that scientists have the last word on how the universe came about. Furthermore, many believe that science has proven that biblical creation never happened. What we will attempt to do in the first part of this book, in down-to-Earth language, is demonstrate that the theory of creationism, contrary to popular belief, does line up with scientific discoveries today. We will also demonstrate that the theory of evolution, which many have forgotten *is* only a theory, lacks scientific, empirical evidence on numerous accounts. We will also demonstrate that the universe and life on Earth suggest that an intelligent designer was behind it all.

1   *If Not Creation, Then What?*

Scientists call it the first law of thermodynamics. Isaac Asimov says that "this law is considered the most powerful and most fundamental generalization about the universe that scientists have ever been able to make."[1] What is this law that lies at the base of all modern science? It is the fact that **while you can convert matter to energy (like heat that results from a burning log), you cannot create energy or matter out of nothing**. So, since we know that our universe is made up of matter and energy, we have to face the reality that it had to come from somewhere. Despite the incredible advances of modern science, the fact remains that not one of our scientific theories can even begin to explain where the energy and matter came from in the first place. **Creation is the only plausible theory that anyone has been able to offer.**

2 *There had to be a beginning...*

For centuries scientists argued that the universe was infinite and eternal. If so, many claimed, there was *no beginning* and hence **nothing for a creator to do**. But, we now know that the amount of usable energy in the universe is decreasing. And, scientists agree, if the universe is running down, it cannot be eternal, or infinite. It will have an end just as it had to have had a beginning. Scientists know this principle as the second law of thermodynamics. It is fascinating to know that **science's two most foundational discoveries argue *for* creation, not against it!**

"...if your theory is found to be against the second law of thermodynamics, I can give you no hope; there is nothing for it but to collapse in deepest humiliation."
- Sir Arthur Eddington

3 *A Beginning Requires a Beginner*

It wasn't until the early part of the twentieth century that Newton's model of an infinite and eternal universe was finally scrapped. The final clincher was Albert Einstein's discovery of the general theory of relativity. Einstein's mathematical theory seemed to prove that everything in the universe is moving away from everything else, suggesting that someone or something must have set it in motion in the first place. Although Einstein didn't like it (he was an atheist), his own discovery forced him to admit that the universe had to have a beginning. And, **if there is a beginning, must there not be a beginner?**

 ## 4   *Einstein, Hubble and the Expanding Universe*

When Einstein's general theory of relativity was published in 1917, it was only a concept and no one knew how to test it. But, in that same year, the world's largest telescope was finally ready to be used for observations. Twelve years later in 1929, astronomer Edwin Hubble (after whom today's Hubble Telescope is named) was able to prove that Einstein's theory was indeed correct. What the telescope showed was that all the other galaxies in the universe were indeed moving away from us. It was from these observations that the Big Bang theory was eventually born. Scientists knew that, according to the law of inertia, these galaxies had to have been set in this kind of motion by some external force. And since the galaxies were moving in a manner similar to the results of a bomb explosion, the theory was born that the universe came into being as a result of a Big Bang. **One thing was for sure, the universe had a beginning**.

5   *What Came Before The Big Bang?*

The idea of a big bang does make sense. Many different observational techniques confirm that every galaxy that we can see, is indeed moving away from every other. If all the galaxies are now moving away from each other, there must have been a time in which they were all closer together. In fact, according to Einstein's mathematical calculations and new scientific discoveries, everything that makes up the universe was at one time so compacted that it did not take up any space whatsoever! While this may be difficult to even begin to imagine, the theory suggests that it eventually exploded, shooting the universe out just as a bomb would. According to this widely accepted theory, the expansion of the universe that we are witnessing today is simply the result of that explosion.

However, **Stephen Hawking, one of the world's leading authorities on the cosmos, admits that this theory does not even try to answer the question of where we, and the rest of the universe came from in the first place.**

6   *Isn't This Theory Backwards?*

The Big Bang theory has become one of the most popular theories for the formation of the universe. There are flaws with the theory, however. For one, **destruction and chaos are the results of an explosion, not systematic order**. A building contractor, for example, would not put all of his materials in a big pile along with a few sticks of dynamite, ignite the dynamite, and then expect the result to be a perfectly constructed office building. But this is what the Big Bang theory is essentially suggesting, that the ordered life we see today was the result of an explosion.

7   *Who Laid Down the Law?*

Some have argued that the order of the universe was created by the laws of gravity. Essentially, this proposal suggests that the force of gravity pulls and holds together, in a delicate balance, all of the stars, planets, asteroids, galaxies etc. So what these scientists are claiming then, is that what started out as chaos was brought into line by the law of gravity. The creationist would have to ask where this law of gravity, and other natural laws, came from in the first place. Are these scientists suggesting that natural laws have some kind of mystical powers in themselves? And **why would there be orderly laws in a universe which just moments before randomly appeared out of chaos?**

8   *Scientists Prove Beginning*

In 1992 there was great excitement over the findings of a team of astrophysicists who had been researching the latest discoveries of COBE (Cosmic Background Explorer), a sophisticated satellite in orbit around the Earth. Scientists had long claimed that if the Big Bang theory was correct, then there would have to be "ripples" or temperature variations in the background radiation of the universe. Astrophysicists claimed that COBE found these long-lost ripples. Now the Big Bang theory is still a theory of course, but the findings are of tremendous importance to Biblical creationists since they **confirm once again that the universe had a beginning**. Indeed, even many non-theistic astronomers had to draw some theistic conclusions about the discoveries. Stephen Hawking, a mathematics professor at Cambridge University and one of the most brilliant men in the world, claimed, "It is the discovery of the century, if not all time."[2] Michael Turner of the Fermi National Accelerator Laboratory near Chicago noted, "The significance of this cannot be overstated. They have found the Holy Grail of cosmology."[3] George Smoot, project leader for COBE noted, "What we have found is evidence for the birth of the universe."[4] The main point is, **if the universe had a beginning, it must have a beginner.**

"For the scientist who has lived by his faith in the power of reason, the story [of the Big Bang] ends like a bad dream. For the past three hundred years, scientists have scaled the mountain of ignorance and as they pull themselves over the final rock, they are greeted by a band of theologians who have been sitting there for centuries."

- Robert Jastrow, Columbia University Professor and Founder of the Goddard Space Center.

9   *Why Does the Universe Have Some Warmer Spots?*

Through the laws of physics we know that heat always flows from hot bodies to cold bodies until they reach a state of balance. If the universe had always been here, then the heat in the universe would be evenly dispersed throughout. But it is not. So, the universe has been here for a period of time less than the redistribution of heat would have taken.

10   *Scientists at Wits End*

Scientists have no idea how the universe began. Indeed, in 1995, the world of cosmology was thrown into chaos when Tod Lauer and Marc Postman of the Space Telescope Science Institute in Baltimore produced research that didn't fit with *any* of the common theories on how the universe functions. An article in *Time* magazine stated that the two young astronomers spent a year trying to debunk their own findings because they knew they would create such a brouhaha. From their research they concluded that a few thousand galaxies, including our own, are not expanding in the same orderly fashion as the rest of the universe. *Time* observed, "Astronomers have come up with one theory-busting discovery after another...Nobody can say what the turmoil means—whether the intellectual edifice of modern cosmology is tottering on the edge of collapse or merely feeling growing pains as it works out a few kinks. "If you ask me,' says astrophysicist Michael Turner of the Fermi National Accelerator Laboratory near Chicago, **either we're close to a**

breakthrough, or we're at our wits' end."[5] The *Time* article also went on to point out other "bewildering discoveries...in a barrage of bafflements."

11   *An Act of Faith*

According to the so-called scientific view, the Universe was created by an incredible series of the most unlikely events that can possibly be imagined. There is no data to support this view, other than a desire to avoid the obvious conclusion, that there must have been a creator'. We know from the second law of thermodynamics that any system, left on its own, will break down and decay, not build itself up and become greater and more complex. However, if this is true, then how did the universe manage to do exactly the opposite? This is another question that science has no answer for. In other words, the **whole idea of a Big Bang and a naturally-created universe requires that very thing that scientists accuse Christians of ....faith.**

12   *Time is Really the* Enemy *of Evolution!*

One of the biggest points of contention between creationists and evolutionists is the issue of time. It is only with time that evolution supposedly becomes respectable. **Something that is totally impossible is suddenly considered quite reasonable when you add a clause suggesting that it happened over billions of years.** As

Evolutionist George Wald noted, "Time is in fact the hero of the plot...given so much time the impossible' becomes possible, the possible probable and the probable virtually certain. One has only to wait: time itself performs miracles."[6] However, the laws of science suggest a problem with this idea. Those laws tell us very clearly that with time things degrade. They do not become better. A tree dies and decomposes into the soil, not the other way around. Scientifically speaking then, time is the *enemy* of evolution, not its friend.

13   *How Old is the Universe?*

How do scientists actually go about calculating the age of the universe? For this, two pieces of information are needed: how far away galaxies are already and how fast they're moving apart. The ratio between these figures will supposedly tell us how long the cosmos has been expanding. This is known as the "Hubble Constant". But can astronomers actually come up with an accurate estimate of the age of our universe?

According to David Branch, an astrophysicist at the University of Oklahoma, there are two big problems with this method: "What's the right distance, and what's the right speed?"[7] *Time* magazine noted that "Since accurate distances can be measured only nearby, while useful galaxies are found only deep in space, astronomers do the best they can to bridge the gap. They use the close galaxies to estimate distances to the faraway ones. But the method is inexact, which is why they haven't been able to agree on what the age actually is."[8] For instance, using data collected by the Hubble Space

Telescope, a research team headed by Wendy Freedman at The Carnegie Observatories suggested that the universe was 8 to 12 billion years old. On the other hand, data collected from the Ultraviolet Imaging Telescope, which was carried into orbit with the Endeavor space shuttle, suggested the universe is 14 billion years old. Astronomer Edwin Hubble had calculated it to be 15 to 20 billion years old. Depending on who you ask, astronomers will tell you that the universe is anywhere from 8 to 20 billion years old.

14   *Rocks from Space*

Most scientists today agree that the best estimate of the age of the Earth is somewhere around 4.6 billion years. How did they manage to come up with this figure? Well, they used a technique called radioisotope dating, which is based on precise measurements of the ratio of the various radioactive isotopes found in a rock. We'll examine radioisotope dating more in the next several points to make it clearer, but first let's look at the rock that scientists examined and tested in order to come up with their estimate. The rock they chose was a meteorite. Meteorites of course, are thought to be pieces of another planet that has broken up some time in the past. **The assumption that scientists are making of course, is that these meteorites are the same age as the Earth!** So, even if these rocks are found to be in the vicinity of 4.6 billion years old, **does it really tell us anything about the age of the Earth?** After all, these rocks aren't even from here.

15 · *Fred Flintstone was Safe*

We've all seen falling stars. These are meteors that are steadily falling toward the Earth and burning up in our atmosphere. Those that don't burn up in this way, crash to Earth as meteorites. Curiously, we only find such rocks in the very top levels of the Earth's surface. **If the Earth's sediments were deposited over hundreds of millions of years, as evolutionists believe, we should find meteorites throughout the various levels of sediment on the Earth's surface. But, we don't.**

16 · *Unreliable Evidence?*

Sometimes radioisotope dating produces different results in repeated experiments on the same sample. This was the case for the **Allende meteorite**. For the most part, when there is a case of conflicting age estimates, it is determined that the rock sample must have been contaminated in some way, and *the results from the tests are simply thrown out*. Of course, paleontologists do their best to pre-screen samples for contamination. But by throwing out samples after this pre-screening, they are admitting that **it is possible for contamination to have occurred without being visibly detected**. But how do we know that the results which *are* kept are indeed accurate? And, perhaps more importantly, **how do we know they weren't kept simply because they lined up with what the paleontologist thought they should be?**

17   *Plus or Minus a Few Billion Years*

Tests were conducted on rocks formed from the lava flow of the Hualalai Volcano in Hawaii which erupted between 1800 and 1801. A variety of radioisotope dating methods were used with each test producing different ages *for the same samples*. The age estimates ranged from 140 million to 2.96 billion years. The same was found for Salt Lake Crater on Oahu. One test result dated a rock at 400,000 years. Others produced results ranging from 2.6 million to 3.3 billion. So **radioisotope dating has been found to give ages which are not only incorrect, but which don't even agree with each other** - in fact, they're not even close!

18   *This Dating Method is All Wet*

Studies have also been conducted on rocks formed from lava flows under the ocean to see if water pressure made any difference in dating results. Samples from the Mt. Kilauea lava flow were taken from a depth of 4,680 meters. The eruption occurred about 200 years ago. The test results, using the radioisotope method of potassium to argon, dated the rock at 21, plus or minus 8, million years. Samples taken from 3,420 meters dated it at 12, plus or minus 2, million years. And those taken from a depth of 1,400 meters were dated at zero. **All of the samples were from the same lava flow**.

19   *Proof Inconclusive*

You may be thinking that although there are some problems with this dating method, it still seems to suggest an Earth that is very old, not young as viewed by literal Biblical creationists. But the fact of the matter is, **of all the dating methods available, only a few give ages of millions or billions of years, namely those using radioisotope techniques.**

20   *Houston, we have a "tiny mystery"*

Another evidence for the Young-Earth hypothesis is found in the mystery of polonium-218. We mentioned "daughter" materials earlier (see "It's 11:00, Do You Know Where Your Daughters Are?). Polonium is one of these daughter materials. We also mentioned the markings left behind in a rock from each element as they break down. These are known as pleochroic halos. Each element produces its own unique halo—leaving its "signature" in the rock. Now, because Polonium is a daughter, there must be a source, or parent. For example, when uranium or thorium decay, one of the elements they break down into along the way is polonium. So a polonium pleochroic halo would appear as a circle where the polonium was, even though the polonium itself is now gone. If there is a pleochroic halo for polonium in a rock, there should also be a pleochroic halo for its source, or parent. However, polonium-218 has been found in granite samples without any evidence of a polonium parent.

Polonium-218 has a half-life of 3.05 minutes, but for simplicity, let's call it 3 minutes even. So if you have a kilo of Polonium-218, after three minutes have passed you will have half a kilo, in an another three minutes you will have a quarter of a kilo, and so on. It continues like this for about 10 half-lives, or thirty minutes. Let's say thirty half-lives have gone by, one and a half hours. For the polonium-218 pleochroic halo to have been set in the granite, which is a metamorphic rock that was once molten, without any trace of a parent, seems to suggest that it was the original element in those base rocks. And for the polonium-218 halo to have been left behind in the granite, **means the granite would have to have cooled down in less than ninety minutes**. The rock, while still in a molten state, would have destroyed any traces of the polonium-218 halo. So it appears the Earth could have been created solid, with the element of polonium-218 in it, in an extremely short period of time. While this theory is not without its critics, **evolutionists have come to admit it is a "tiny mystery"**.

21   *Hey, Where are all the People?*

There are many young-Earth evidences that are, while not necessarily definitive, at least compelling. Take, for example, the dating of civilization. Observations of today's population and population growth patterns suggest a young Earth. The human population of the world today is somewhere in the vicinity of 6 billion individuals. The present rate of growth is about 2%. At this rate it would have taken about 1,100 years to reach the present population from the time of the flood. And we, of course, have to take into account that people have died along the way which would make it a bit longer to reach the present population. **If man were around for a million years or so, as evolutionists suggest, the population should be about 10^{8600}. That's a 1 with 8600 zeros following it— a ridiculous number.** The population growth rate, in order to account for present population data, would have to be about 0.002%. But as we just mentioned, today we observe a population growth rate of about 2%. Even in recent years with the development of mass weaponry, brutal genocide, some of the worst wars, plagues and famines in history, and a rampant abortion rate, the population growth rate hasn't changed very much at all.

22   *No Bones About It*

Let's say that the population growth rate was 0.002%, as evolutionary theory would have to suggest. That would mean that **an absolutely unimaginable number of people would have to have lived and died during the last million years or so**. There is *no empirical evidence*, i.e. human remains or bones, to prove that such a vast number of people have ever lived on this Earth over the past million years.

23   *Where's the Stuff?*

Not only are there no bones to demonstrate the existence of the vast number of people that evolution requires (see "No Bones About It"), but their "stuff" is missing too. Where are their tools, cooking implements, homes, weapons etc? A population of this size would certainly have left an almost unbelievable number of artifacts behind when they died.

24 *The Seeds of Intelligence*

It is hard to imagine people, just as intelligent as we are today, living for tens, or even hundreds of thousands of years, without ever discovering that the plants they were eating grew from seeds. And yet, the archaeological record clearly shows that man has been planting his own food for less than 10,000 years! Clearly this suggests that man hasn't been around for as long as evolutionists believe (and require).

25 *Fossils Support Young Earth*

The very fact that fossils exist at all seems to lend support to the idea of a young Earth. This is because, when an animal dies in the wild, its body is devoured by scavengers and disappears within days or weeks. It becomes a fossil only in those cases where it is covered over by sediment very, very quickly. This suggests than **any rock strata that contain fossils, must have been laid down very quickly**.

26 *Venus de Mile High*

Venus is much closer to the sun than the Earth is and so the surface temperature on that planet hovers somewhere close to 1000°F. Had the planets existed for billions of years, then Venus' crust would have heated into a soft tar'. (Remember even hard elements like lead and zinc melt well below 1000 degrees). Yet, when we look at Venus today we see many very tall mountains. In fact, one such mountain, called Maat Mons is even taller than our own Mount Everest! If Venus had been there for billions of years, then the crust of the planet would simply be too soft to support such mountains and they would long ago have simply "oozed" into a big puddle.

27   *Star Light, Star Bright*

There are stars within our galaxy that are burning up much faster than our own sun. These stars are called "O" stars, and they are using up their fuel hundreds of times faster than the sun. The implication of this finding is that these stars must be rather young on an evolutionary scale — otherwise they would have burned themselves out by now. Or, if they were once large enough to support such a rate of disintegration, we should then be seeing the resulting characteristics like high rotation speeds and huge magnetic fields. But such tell-tale signs do not exist.

28   *Evolution Finds Magnetic Field Unattractive'*

The Earth's magnetic field also provides support for the idea of a young Earth. A strong magnetic field is crucial for life as we know it. It forms a protective covering around the Earth, blocking it from harmful cosmic radiation that continuously bombards the Earth. Observations made of the Earth's magnetic field over the last century and a half have shown that it is measurably decreasing in intensity. **Since 1829 it has been measured that the strength of the magnetic field has decreased by about 7%.** It has been calculated that the half-life of the magnetic field is about 1,400 years, meaning it decays to half its strength every fourteen hundred years. If it gets too weak life will not be possible. **If the Earth was as old as evolutionists claim, the magnetic field would be non-existent by now.**

29 *A 20,000 Year Limit on Life*

Let's look at the Earth's magnetic field *backward* in time. We know that according to half-life calculations, the magnetic field must have been twice as strong as it is now about 1,400 years ago. If we went back in time then, say 100,000 years, that field would have been unbelievably strong, and **life would simply not have been possible**. In fact, it has been calculated by Dr. Thomas Barnes, former Dean of the Institute for Creation Research and Graduate School, and Emeritus Profess of Physics at the University of Texas in El Paso, that at **any time beyond 20,000 years ago life, as we know it, would have been impossible on Earth.**

30 *An Airtight Argument*

Another young Earth argument centers around the presence of helium in the Earth's atmosphere. Helium is an extremely light gas. In fact, only hydrogen is lighter. By comparing the percentage of helium in the atmosphere to the total volume of the atmosphere, scientists are able to calculate the total number of helium atoms that must be present there. Since helium is produced below the Earth's surface, and escapes from there into the atmosphere—scientists should be able to use the rate of that escape to calculate the age of the atmosphere itself. Dr. Larry Vardiman, Chairman of the Physics Department at the Institute for Creation Research has done extensive work on this and has produced an "airtight" argument.[9] He **calculated that the amount of helium in the atmosphere would have accumulated in no more than two million years**. Now, while young-Earth creationists may not like this old date, it is still younger than the widely accepted age of the universe and the Earth in the scientific community. We should also note that these calculations were based on the assumption that the rate of accumulation of helium in the atmosphere has never changed. And it also assumes that when the Earth was formed there were *no* helium atoms present in the atmosphere to begin with. But **if the Earth were designed to sustain life by a Creator, it is likely He would have had helium present in the atmosphere right from the start. This would obviously bring the time needed for the present accumulation down**.

31   *Another Helium Mystery*

The release of helium into the atmosphere has been measured at thirteen million helium atoms per square inch per second. There is still a vast amount of helium below the Earth's crust. Because helium is so lightweight there is no rock that is able to block its escape into the atmosphere. Now, radioactive decay in rocks does replenish some of the helium below the surface, but not enough to account for the amount there. If the process of helium escaping into the atmosphere had been going on for billions of years, **there should be a lot more helium in the atmosphere than there is and a lot less below the Earth's surface**. So not only does the small amount of helium in the atmosphere support a young-Earth view, so does the vast amount of helium still sitting below the Earth's crust.

32   *Take Evolution with A Grain of Salt*

Evolutionists believe that life began in a salty ocean around 3 to 4 billion years ago. Supporters of the young-Earth view, however, point out the fact that if the Earth is as old as evolutionists say it is, then the oceans should be a lot saltier than they are today. Studies have been conducted by Dr. Steve Austin and Russell Humphreys[10] on the rate at which sodium is deposited into and taken out of the oceans. Austin and Humphreys determined that **the Earth could not be older than 62 million years, much younger than evolutionists claim**. Now, while young-Earth creationists may not like this age, it must be remembered that Austin and Humphreys used the most extreme conditions for input and the least extreme conditions for output to be more than fair to the evolutionist view point. Regardless, it *was* determined that the amount of salt going into the oceans is greater than the amount going out. So, even if the oceans came into existence with no salt in them, they should now be much saltier than they actually are.

33 *Our Shrinking Sun*

Over the past 150 years, astronomers have made careful, regular measurements of the sun's diameter and have shown that our sun is shrinking at a rate of about 5 feet per hour. Extending the implications of these observations we can only conclude that **had the sun existed several million years ago, it would have been so much bigger than it is today that its heat would have made life on Earth impossible.** This flies in the face of evolutionary theory which suggests that a million years ago all the life we see today was already here. In fact, a million years is not that long ago by evolutionary standards, with the process believed to have begun hundreds of millions or even billions of years ago!

34 *Enjoy the View, while you can!*

The rings that wrap around Saturn are being rapidly bombarded by meteoroids. Some calculations estimate that such pulverization would destroy the rings completely in about 10,000 years. Since the rings are still there, the implication is that the rings around Saturn are quite a bit younger than evolutionists believe.

35 *Houston, How far did you say it was to the Moon?*

The rotation of the Earth is slowing down. This is caused by the friction' of the tides and it has been observed since the 1700's. We know from physics that this means that the Moon is slowly moving away from us. But, even if the Moon began orbiting right at the Earth's surface, it would still be much further away from us than it is if this process indeed started some 4.6 billion years ago.

36 *Why Don't You Just Cool Down?*

Jupiter, Saturn, and Neptune each give off twice as much heat as the sun provides. Since it is not believed that these planets build up heat through nuclear fusion, radioactive decay or gravitational contraction, the only other conceivable explanation is that these planets have not existed long enough to cool off.

37 Finding the Dirt on *Evolutionary Theory*

Every time it rains, or the winds pick up, more of the continents are eroded away, and the soil is washed out to sea. In fact, studies have shown that close to 25 billion tons of sediment are removed from dry land and deposited in the ocean every year. At that rate, it would take less than 20 million years to completely erode the continents so that no dry land remained above sea level. If we accept evolution as the explanation for life on Earth, then certainly we have to wonder why there is still dry land if the evolutionary process has been going on, on dry land, for *hundreds of millions* of years.

At the same time, **after hundreds of millions of years one would expect to find several miles of sediment on the ocean floors around the world. In reality, we see only hundreds of feet of sediment,** again suggesting a much younger world than evolutionists would have us believe.

38 *That Sinking Feeling*

When men were preparing to land on the Moon for the first time, there was concern about the dust that they would find there. In fact, based on their assumption that the universe was billions of years old, experts feared that the astronauts might simply sink into as much as a mile of dust on the surface of the Moon! This of course, did not happen and scientists were forced to reconsider the age of the Moon when they found only a very thin layer of dust.

39 *Would you believe Mount Rushmore was an Accident?*

Imagine walking through the forest and coming across a tree with the words "Fred loves Wilma" carved into the trunk. Would you assume that those words had formed there by accident? Of course not. What about Mount Rushmore? Do you think anyone who sees it for the first time thinks that those faces simply appeared through erosion and other natural processes? You see, one thing we seem to have a pretty good sense about in every day life is determining what was man-made and what was a natural occurance. In other words, **our experience tells us quite readily what nature is capable of producing and what requires the intervention of an intelligent designer**. At the same time however, we see evolutionists looking at some of the most astonishing designs imaginable, and suggesting that they are all just happy accidents.

40   *Careful Design or Wonderful Accident?*

      Perhaps the best, and most striking evidence for the existence of a designer is the **complexity of the design** itself. Take for example the co-dependent relationship between the Pronuba moth and the Yucca plant, both of which naturally reside in the desert. The Yucca plant's very existence is dependent upon the Pronuba moth, whose eggs hatch in the desert sand at the base of the plant. Interestingly, this only happens on certain nights of the year, when the flowers of the Yucca plant are in bloom. You see, the moth, which is also dependent on the Yucca plant for *its* very life, takes pollen from one of the plant's flowers, and then flies to a different Yucca plant to lay its eggs. When it arrives at the other plant, the moth first pushes the pollen that it has collected from the first plant, into a flower on the second plant. That plant will then grow and prosper, fertilizing the moth eggs in the sand at its base. Her task complete, the Pronuba moth dies that same night. When the eggs hatch, the caterpillars will build cocoons at the base of the plant, and wait their turn to repeat this incredible cycle of survival. Equally amazing is the fact that there are several varieties of Yucca plant, and each one is pollinated by its own species of moth. **How could all these varieties of the moth and Yucca plant have randomly come into coordinated existence, and then randomly evolved in perfect coordination just to give each other life?**

41 *Evidence of Design*

Obviously one of the most important elements in the discussion of a Creator, is the beginning of life itself. So, let's now step back in time to the very first appearance of primitive life on Earth. Not surprisingly, the creation of life was a complex process, requiring countless combinations of the elements of the universe to come together in a very precise way. For example, atoms of varying degrees of size must form. But before this can happen, there needs to be a precise balance of various other constants in the physical world, such as gravity, nuclear forces, the proper expansion rate of the universe, and the proper ratio of electrons and protons, to name just a few. In many of the myriad of variables in this complex equation, a change as small as one tenth of one percent could make life impossible. Such precision seems to suggest that **there was great care taken in making the universe a place capable of supporting life**. Indeed, many scientists today now admit that the universe seems to have been *specially crafted for life*.

42   *Words of Wisdom from the Scientific Community*

"The origin of life appears to be almost a miracle, so many are the conditions which would have had to be satisfied to get it going." [11]

"It would be very difficult to explain why the universe should have begun in just this way, except as the act of a God who intended to create beings like us." [12]

43   *A Delicate Balance*

There are many known factors that must be precisely met in order for life to exist here on Earth. Any slight variation, in any of these factors, would spell disaster. The rate of the Earth's rotation for example, is ideal. If it were to slow down to 10% of its present rate, then life as we know it could not exist. Plants would burn during the day, and then freeze during the night. If on the other hand the rotation were to speed up too much winds would increase to unbelievable levels. In fact, Jupiter rotates on its axis once every 10 hours and the winds there are in excess of 1000 MPH! So again, we see great precision in the design of the Earth, and that is what allows it to support life. And **when you see all of these evidences of design, you must logically expect there to be a designer**.

44 *The Glue That Binds Us All*

There is a powerful force within the universe, holding together all the atoms and making the various elements (Hydrogen, Helium, Oxygen, Iron etc.) possible. If however, this force was even 5% weaker, then the only element that could exist on Earth would be Hydrogen and that would make life impossible. At the same time, if that same force were just 5% stronger, everything would clump together into giant molecules. Life would also be impossible under these conditions.

45 *The Stars of Creation*

Something that is absolutely astonishing, is the realization that all of those stars we see in the night sky (and trillions that we don't see) are <u>necessary</u> for life to be possible here on Earth! In fact, if there were too many stars, our own sun could not have survived. If there were too few stars on the other hand, the heavy elements necessary for life, would never have formed in the first place.

46 *Expansion Speed Just So*

Sure the universe is expanding, but this only proves that there must have been a beginning. And fortunately for us, that beginning was perfectly arranged and planned. You see, if the universe expanded more quickly than it does now, then matter would simply spread out too fast and planets and galaxies would never have formed. If on the other hand, the universe expanded more slowly, then it wouldn't have been able to overcome the tremendous gravity of all that matter and everything in it would simply have collapsed into one giant clump.

47 *Thank God! The Sun is Right Where is Should Be*

The distance between the Earth and the sun is about 93 million miles. Did you realize that if this distance were changed by only 2% in either direction, life on Earth would be impossible. At the same time, our Moon is right where it needs to be to both stabilize the tilt of the Earth and to cleanse and nourish the sea through tides. In fact, if the Moon were too close, then the tides would completely submerge the continents, twice a day.

48 *Gasp!*

The air that you are breathing right now contains approximately 21% oxygen. If that ratio were to rise even slightly, say to 25%, then our atmosphere would suddenly become highly flammable. If it were to fall to 15% or less, then you simply wouldn't be able to breathe and you'd suffocate immediately.

49 *I'm Stuck on this Planet*

Gravity is what keeps us all pinned to the ground, and like so many other natural phenomena, it has been set up perfectly. If the Earth's gravitational pull were to be increased just a few percent, then some of the most dangerous gases in our atmosphere would accumulate and make life impossible (ie Methane and Ammonia). Reducing the gravitational pull would result in the loss of too much water.

50   *Space Brothers?*

Seeing the overwhelming evidence of design, many have suggested that it does indeed seem impossible for such precise conditions to have somehow come together completely by chance. But rather than see it as evidence for the existence of God, some are now suggesting that life on Earth was planted here by beings from outer space. This theory is called panspermia, but it fails to answer the question of where life *actually began.* In other words, where did the aliens come from?

51   *Are We Alone in the Universe?*

One of the biggest questions on the minds of people today, is whether or not life is unique to Earth. Research conducted by Iosef Shklovski and Carl Sagan in the mid-1960s found that it took a very special kind of star, at just the right distance from a planet, for life to exist. They calculated that only 0.001% of the stars can have a planet that is capable of sustaining advanced life. Later research showed there are even fewer. According to Christian astrophysicist Hugh Ross, Ph.D., "it is possible, even at this stage in the research efforts, to gather many of the planetary system parameters for life support and determine a crude estimate for the possibility that by natural means alone there would exist a planet capable of supporting life...with considerable security, we can draw the conclusion that **much fewer than a trillionth of a trillionth of a percent of all stars could possibly possess, without divine intervention, a planet capable of sustaining advanced life**. Considering that the observable universe contains less than a trillion galaxies, each averaging a hundred billion stars, we can see **that not even one planet would be expected, by natural processes alone, to possess the necessary conditions to sustain life**."[13]

52 *Pie in the Sky*

Of course, many evolutionists have hoped that life would be discovered on other planets since this would help prove their theory that life *can* occur randomly under the right conditions. In 1976 there was great hope and expectation that the *Viking* mission to Mars would reveal life on what was thought to be the only other planet in our solar system capable of sustaining life. Four different intricate experiments, using extremely sensitive equipment, were conducted on Martian soil. The conclusion? Mars was not capable of supporting life.

53 | The Two-Faced Question of Design

Today, the tireless search continues for signs of extraterrestrial life. Millions and millions of dollars have been spent setting up huge satellite dishes, pointed into the sky, **listening for messages from outer space.** Ironically, when you ask those people who are actually doing the listening how they will know that a sound they hear is indeed an intelligent signal, they will tell you that it will have a pattern or design to it. Many of these same people however, can somehow **look at creation, with all of its intelligent patterns and evidences of design, and tell us that it simply came about by random chance!**

54 | The <u>Miracle</u> of Life

Clearly we can't really consider the design of life without looking very closely at the incredible complexity and design of living organisms. Take for example, the very cells that make up our bodies. There are over one trillion such cells in the human body, with each one being made up of components which interact with each other in a very precise and extremely complex way. Protein molecules for example, conduct, individually or in groups, all of the necessary tasks to ensure the life of a cell. Proteins contain long chain-like molecules made up of amino acids. And every different protein has a unique linear sequence of amino acids. Also, most proteins are made up of several thousand atoms which form different three-dimensional infrastructures for different tasks. It is difficult to fathom how each of these individual components randomly evolved in the first place, and then somehow miraculously came together to form a living cell.

55 Life's Really Little Instruction Book

Looking at individual protein molecules, we see incredible variety, with each individual molecule having a very specific task in life. So how do these molecules know what that task is? That information can be found in other molecules, known as DNA and RNA. **These incredible molecules actually carry the instructions for creating life**. DNA contains the actual blueprint for building life molecules, and RNA carries that information to other parts of the cell. You can think of DNA as being like a compact disk full of information, and the RNA as the CD player. Without the RNA, the cells would have no way of understanding the information contained in the DNA—information that will tell the protein molecules to form or repair living cells! Even more staggering however, is the fact that the instructions for building RNA are contained in the DNA. It would be like having a CD that contained all of the instructions detailing how to build a CD player. But with no CD player to play it on, how could you ever get those instructions out?

Again we can't help but see clear signs of intelligent design and the impossibility of life coming about purely by chance.

56   *How Can Trial and Error Work When Error is Fatal?*

The study of the human body is one of the most clear evidences for the existence of an intelligent designer. Take the kidney for example. Here is an organ so complex that even minor fluctuations in its functioning can be fatal. And yet evolutionists would have us believe that this incredible organ simply evolved and developed through trial and error. We all know that trial and error is not a reliable method for problem solving, but how much less so when you consider that errors will kill the organism and end the entire trial and error process.

57   *The Ultimate Computer*

Think about the most complex organ of the them all—the human brain. Here we have a lump of grey matter, made up of somewhere close to ten thousand million nerve cells. Now consider the fact that each of these cells is comprised of anywhere from ten thousand to one hundred thousand connecting fibers. Each of these fibers, in turn, makes contact with other nerve cells in the brain, **giving each of us about one thousand million million possible connections**. Such a number is beyond the reach of our wildest imagination and becomes even more staggering when we consider the fact that these connections are not just random occurrences. They are arranged in an intricate and extremely precise network. It's difficult to conceive of such complexity and perfection coming about by accident.

58   *The Human Brain*

How many times have you heard people talking about how small a percentage of our brain power we actually use? Well, next time someone mentions that, there's an important question that you should raise. How is it is possible, using the theory of evolution, to explain this? Natural selection sure can't explain it since those very capabilities were never used (by definition) and so could not possibly have provided any survival advantage.

59   *The Eyes Have It*

Perhaps the most conclusive quote on the matter of creation versus evolution comes from the father of the evolutionary theory, Charles Darwin. When considering the design of the eye for example, Darwin noted, "To suppose that the eye with all its inimitable contrivances for adjusting the focus to different distances, for admitting different amounts of light, and for the correction of spherical and chromatic aberration, could have formed by natural selection, seems, I freely confess, absurd in the highest degree."[14] And He was right. There are over 10 million light sensitive cells packed tightly together in the retina of the human eye. Equally astounding is the fact that these cells have a very high rate of metabolism and are completely destroyed and replaced about once a week! More staggering, is the fact that each of these cells is vastly more complex than even the most sophisticated computer. In fact, it is believed that the retina conducts close to 10 billion (that's

10,000,000,000) calculations every second, and that's before the image even gets to the brain! Here is what was written about the eye in the computer magazine BYTE. "To simulate 10 milliseconds of the complete processing of even a single nerve cell from the retina would require the solution of about 500 simultaneous non-linear differential equations one hundred times and would take at least several minutes of processing time on a Cray supercomputer. Keeping in mind that there are 10 million or more such cells interacting with each other in complex ways it would take a minimum of a hundred years of Cray time to simulate what takes place in your eye many times every second." It's hard to imagine such a system coming about by chance and accident. It's easier to understand God's word when it tells us "The hearing ear and the seeing eye, the Lord hath made even both of them." (Proverbs 20:12)

60   *Darwin's Theory*

In 1831 Charles Darwin set sail on the Beagle, and on this voyage, he took note of various species of plants, insects, and wildlife that were distinct, yet closely related. Among the most famous of Darwin's observed species were "Darwin's finches". He noted that there were fourteen species of this bird in the Galapagos Islands, all of which appeared to have come from a common ancestor. The varieties that exist there today differ mainly in minor characteristics like the size and shape of the bill. The important thing to realize however, is that all the new finches are still finches. They did not become owls, eagles, or turkey vultures. Nor did they become a whole new species, evolving into monkeys, kangaroos or prairie dogs. In other words, despite all the weight given to Darwin's observations of these finches, there is nothing there that adds any credibility at all to Darwin's theory that all life evolved from a common ancestor.

Today, Darwin's theory has been chalked up as a rebuttal to the creation account found in the Bible, but in reality, it is no such thing. First of all, the doctrine of fixity of species was a man-made doctrine, and has absolutely nothing to do with the Biblical account. The Bible does not say that God only created one type of finch in the first place, nor does it say that different types of finches which may have migrated from different geographical areas cannot breed together. The important thing to understand is this: For the most part, **Darwin's *observations* are not in question, but his *conclusions* are.**

61 *An Introduction to Homology*

Another major foundation of Darwin's belief in evolution (although he did have some doubts) was the amazing similarity in the anatomy of living organisms. He compared, for example, the similarities in the construction of a man's hand, a porpoise's paddle, and a bat's, or a bird's, wing. This is known as homology. Such similarities in homology suggested to him that each of these creatures must have inherited these characteristics from a common ancestor. Homology has always been, and remains today, a key element of the theory of evolution. If homologous characteristics could have been demonstrated to have been passed on through genetics and embryological development, the case for evolution could certainly have been strengthened. But this has not been the case. **In fact, there is no genetic or embryological basis for homology whatsoever**. Clearly, while the phenomenon of homology may be a key pillar in the theory of evolution, it is a very shaky pillar indeed.

62 *Works For Me*

Darwin asked his critics, and evolutionists still ask today, "Why would such an intelligent creator as God be limited to using similar designs in different species of animals?" There is a very good answer to this question. Why does man stick to similar designs for car engines for all automobiles, whether produced by Chrysler, Ford, or Toyota? For one reason - **because it's a design that works**!

"A professor at Johns Hopkins has come forth with an intriguing thought about a perennial question: he says that if an infinite number of monkeys sat typing at an infinite number of typewriters, the smell in the room would be unbearable."

-David Letterman

63 *Where's the Link?*

The classification of species, based on similarities, like those of the anatomy, is known as taxonomy. Taxonomy, through the years, has shown that species are divided into distinct classes, with *no transitional sequences* being apparent. Recently, the advent of molecular biology has added a whole new chapter to the field of taxonomy. It has been found, for example, that the blood chemical, hemoglobin, varies between species. Differences in protein can also be used to measure the differences between species. So we see that scientists are not only able to separate species on the basis of anatomy, but on the basis of molecular differences as well. Further, **molecular biology, like anatomical biology, shows no evidence of intermediate species**. In other words, molecular biologists have found no evidence to support the evolutionist's claim that fish evolved into amphibians, which evolved into reptiles, which evolved into mammals.

64   *Survival of the Fittest?*

When Darwin was first developing his theory, he was unable to come up with an answer to the key question of what caused a species to change (i.e. evolve) in the first place. After some effort, he came up with his theory of "survival of the fittest", suggesting that more individuals of each species were being produced than the environment could support. The theory suggests that members of the species that possessed slight advantages over the others would be more likely to survive and pass on their genetic makeup to their offspring. The giraffe's long neck for example evolved gradually over time, allowing the animals to reach higher and higher into the trees for food, especially during times of famine. Through the process of "**natural selection**", the giraffes with the longest necks were best equipped to survive and hence pass on their "long neck" genes to future generations. But how would accidental variations be preserved within a species? Darwin didn't know it at the time, but today biologists now possess a model of genetic inheritance that demonstrates how a genetic trait can be passed over several generations and influence an entire population. While this may appear to support the evolution argument, it really doesn't. You see, **not all traits are passed on through genetics**. The children of a father born with three fingers are no more likely than anyone else to be born with three fingers. At the same time, experiments in breeding domestic animals have proven that some species do indeed undergo some degree of change, but there is an outer limit to change. Just as with Darwin's finches, the cross between a Cocker Spaniel and a Poodle becomes a Cock-a-Poo. **But it is still a dog, not a giraffe.**

65 *The Greatest Gift*

Countless people throughout history have endangered or even sacrificed their lives for another. Even some animals will do this. This reality is completely at odds with Darwin's theory of the survival of the fittest.

66 *Where's the Advantage in This?*

Evolution cannot explain how intermediary species survived between stages. For example, we are told that birds evolved from reptiles and that the scales common to reptiles evolved, over millions of years, into feathers. A bird's wing and feathers are, of course, designed with absolute perfection in order to make flight possible. The feathers have to be of a specific strength. They have to be capable of withstanding deformation. And there has to be <u>exactly</u> the right amount of feathers in order for flight to occur. Thinking about this scenario, it is very difficult to imagine the process continuing through natural selection as the reptile's scales become **less useful** to them (as they begin to look more like feathers) as the animal evolves into a bird with deformed wings that don't even function as such. **There appears to be no "environmental** *advantage"* **at any stage in the process, and in fact, there seem to be considerable** *disadvantages*! .

67 | *Darwin, You Take My Breath Away!*

As evolutionists argue that birds evolved from reptiles, there is another problem to consider—respiration. There are no other known vertebrate species on Earth that have a lung system similar to that found in birds. The question then, is **how the intermediate species that must have existed between reptiles and birds managed to survive with a malfunctioning respiratory system** that would surely result in immediate death to the creature. When you really sit down and think about it, many of the key premises upon which evolutionary theory are based seem utterly ridiculous.

68 The Jet and the Junkyard

Not only did Darwin believe that natural selection was a method of survival, he also believed that evolutionary changes came about as random chance occurrences. Yet, if you were to pick up a pencil and ask someone where it originated, they would likely tell you that someone made it. It would be absolutely silly for them to suggest that it came about through a series of highly unlikely and random events in the universe. But that is the very argument presented by evolutionists. Sir Fred Hoyle is one of the world's leading astronomers and mathematicians. Although he is not a creationist, he did have this to say about evolution to an audience at the British Academy of Science: "Let's be scientifically honest. We all know that **the probability of life arising to greater and greater complexity and organization by chance through evolution is the same probability as having a tornado tear through a junkyard and form out the other end a Boeing 747 jetliner!**"[15] In mathematical terms, he calculated the chances of life just happening by random chance to be one in $10^{40,000}$. That's a one with 40,000 zeroes following it! For perspective, consider the following examples.

A one in a million chance is one in 10^6
The distance around the Earth is 10^9 inches!
The visible universe is about 10^{28} inches in diameter!

69 Evolution is Against the Law

All observations, from the earliest beginnings of time right up to the present, have shown over and over again that *life only comes from life*. Period. So fundamental is this reality in fact that it is called the **Law of Biogenesis**, and it has **never been violated** under observation or experimentation. Clearly however, the theory of evolution would require the violation of this law in order to suggest that life somehow came into existence from purely non-living matter, by purely natural processes.

70   *Soup's On!*

       Despite such enormous odds against the sudden appearance of life by completely random chance, evolutionists still argue for this point. They tell us that before life there was nothing but what they call a "prebiotic soup", basically a great big puddle of chemicals. This soup contained a mixture of organic and inorganic molecules, that somehow, just found itself in random possession of all the conditions necessary to create life—which it did. **From that accident, from that most unlikely of events, somehow everything on this planet evolved, including palm trees, Basset Hounds and Elvis Presley.** This not only sounds absurd, it also violates the law of biogenesis which tells us that life can only come from life. A number of years ago a molecular biologist named Harold Morowitz determined that if one were to break down a 'simple' cell according to its chemical bonds, the cell could not reform even under the most ideal natural conditions. In fact, he calculated the likelihood of reassembly to be one chance in $10^{100,000,000,000,000}$. A number of attempts have been made by scientists to create a "prebiotic soup" and apply all of the ideal conditions for life to develop. Of course, none of these experiments have been successful in creating life.

71   *Where's The Beef?*

You would think that evidence for the existence of the so-called prebiotic soup from which life first appeared would be critical to the theory of evolution. Surprisingly though, this theory exists with no such evidence. In fact, while it would seem feasible to expect that remnants from such a prebiotic soup should have been trapped in rocks from those early days—**no such remnant has ever been found**. Even rocks which are, according to geologists, close to 3,900 million years old show no traces of this prebiotic soup. Even so, its existence has become widely accepted as truth!

72   *Too Much Oxygen Spoils the Broth*

Not only is there no empirical evidence for a prebiotic soup, there are other problems with the concept in theory as well. It has been determined for example, that any organic substances formed in the early days of the Earth would have been quickly oxidized and destroyed in the presence of oxygen. Thus, **these organic compounds would simply not have survived long enough to be able to accumulate into a prebiotic soup**—let alone long enough for life to 'spring into existence'.

73 *A Hole In The Ozone Theory*

Some have suggested that Earth's early environment must not have contained any oxygen, meaning that the simple organic compounds could have avoided destruction by oxidization. Even if it were true that there was no oxygen at the time, that would mean that there would have been no ozone layer in the Earth's upper atmosphere as there is today. **Without that protective layer of ozone, lethal radiation from the sun would have destroyed any organic compounds that may have existed**.

74 *A Leap in Logic*

Prior to the 1950s, evolutionists hoped that science would one day be able to provide signs of intermediate steps between non-living molecules and the simplest cell. In other words, scientists were hoping to show that life could have indeed come about spontaneously, from purely non-living matter. However, since the rise of molecular biology in the early 1950s it has been shown that there are *no intermediate forms* leading to the evolution of a simple cell from chemical synthesis. Life comes from life. Period. (See "Evolution is Against the Law"). Nor is there evidence for a primitive simple cell evolving into the complex cells we have today.

75 There is No Such Thing as a Simple Life Form

Evolutionists tell us that we came from some type of simple cell like an amoebae. What do we know about the amoebae? It is a one-celled animal that can crawl towards food. If necessary it can produce a pseudopod, a false foot, to propel itself towards the food. When the foot is no longer needed it disappears. The amoebae has chromosomes, genes and DNA. Its method of reproduction is an extremely complicated and precise process. So, even the lowly amoebae, which at first may appear to be an unbelievably simple life organism, is upon closer examination found to be quite complex. Evolution cannot even begin to answer the question of how this seemingly simple cell developed without some intelligent planning and design behind it.

76 Forget the Doctor, Get me an Electrician

Within the fabric of life, we find the most complex systems we've ever encountered or created. These include electrical, acoustical, mechanical, chemical, and optical systems. These systems are so complex that we cannot even copy them. Such phenomena include the sonar systems of dolphins, porpoises, and whales; the frequency-modulated radar and discrimination system of the bat; the control systems, internal ballistics, and combustion chamber of the bombardier beetle; the aerodynamic capabilities of the hummingbird; the complex and redundant navigational systems of many birds and fish; and especially the self-repair capabilities of practically all forms of life.

77   *Now that's Efficient!*

Tiny bacteria, such as Salmonella, Escherichia coli, and some Streptococci, are able to propel themselves at speeds of up to 15 body lengths per second. They do this with microscopic reversible motors that can spin at 100,000 revolutions per minute. These little motors whirl a bundle of flagella that act as a propeller. The power for this motor comes in the form of electrical charges just like in the case of a man-made motor. Today the Japanese are spending millions trying to learn how these motors work. Why the interest? Eight million of these bacterial motors would fit on the head of a pin! It is funny that the evolutionary theory argues that bacteria such as these were among the 'simple cells' that evolved first.

78   *A Book that Writes Itself!*

One simple cell is so much more complex than our most powerful computers that it boggles the mind. Carl Sagan says that there are about 10^{12} bits of information in each one. He illustrates that by saying that it is **the equivalent of about 100 million pages of the Encyclopedia Brittanica.** How likely is it that this is the result of random chance?

79   *The Lottery You Can't Win*

The code in the average cell is equivalent to about 100 million pages of the Encyclopedia Brittanica. Each part of the puzzle has to go in a specific sequence or the whole cell dies. Now consider the following illustration. If you put ten scrabble letters into a hat that, if arranged properly, would spell R-E-P-U-B-L-I-C-A-N, you would have a one in 3,628,800 chance of pulling the letters out, one at a time, in exactly the right order. If we were to try another experiment, this time starting with each of the 26 letters of the alphabet, and then trying to pull them out in alphabetical order, the odds of getting it right are only one in 403 trillion trillion. That's one chance in 403,000,000,000,000,000,000,000,000,000. **Now imagine the odds of randomly getting 100 million pages of information in perfect order!**

80   *The Mystery of the Simple Cell*

A typical living cell contains thousands of different chemicals that would react with others if they came into contact. Yet, cells are filled with intricate systems of chemical barriers and buffers to prevent this from happening. If cells evolved, that would mean that these walls would also have to have evolved. But, how did the cells, with all these chemicals inside them, avoid the deadly chemical reactions until the walls were all built?

81   *Try to Figure the Logic in this...*

Doesn't it seem strange that brilliant men could spend their entire lives in a lab trying to create life just to show that NO INTELLIGENCE was necessary to form it in the first place. For hundreds of years brilliant men have been **trying - and failing**

- to make even the simplest life, and yet those same men would have you believe that life began through nothing more than time and chance.

82 *The First Step?*

Evolutionists have some difficulty in answering questions about the amoebae's reproduction. The amoebae, when it reproduces, still reproduces its own kind. It does not produce another life form. Neither does it produce male or female. So, how, when and why did the amoebae evolve into different genders and even different, higher life forms?

83 *Evolution and Mutation*

One thing that evolutionists have to admit is that mutations are the *only source of new genetic information* for natural selection to work on. Webster's dictionary defines a mutation as "a sudden departure from the parent type in one or more heritable characteristics, caused by a change in a gene or a chromosome." Dr. H.J. Muller, who won the Nobel prize for his work on mutations said that "It is entirely in line with the accidental nature of mutations that extensive tests have agreed in showing the vast majority of them detrimental to the organism in its job of surviving and reproducing. **Good ones are so rare we can consider them all bad.**" (Bulletin of the Atomic Scientists, 11:331). It is important to remember, that in order for a mutation to be passed on to future generations, it must occur in the sperm or egg cells of the parent. The probability of getting even five mutations in the same cell is estimated to be 1 chance in

100,000,000,000,000,000,000,000. If there was a population of 100 million organisms, with a reproductive cycle of 1 day, such an event would occur once every 274 billion years! Again, it requires more faith to believe in those odds, than it does to believe in a creator.

84 *Remember, it's the Theory of Evolution!*

Critics of creationism claim that the Genesis account of creation can never be proven by science. This is true. But the same holds true for Darwin's theory of evolution. Many seem to have forgotten that evolution is only a theory, not a scientific fact. It is treated in textbooks, science journals, classrooms and TV documentaries as fact and this has led to its perceived credibility. But one thing is clear, the theory of evolution is filled with theoretical, logical, and scientific errors. Accepting this theory requires as much, if not more faith than accepting the creation account.

85 *I Guess That's Why They're Called Missing Links*

The fossil record is often shown in textbooks as a tree trunk with branches growing out from it. While the fossil tree shows horizontal branches which demonstrate the supposed mutation of species into other species, there is absolutely no empirical evidence to support the existence of such horizontal branches. In other words there is no evidence in the fossil record to support the existence of any intermediary species. These are known as **missing** links, and yet even though they are missing, they are the cornerstone of the entire theory of evolution.

86 *Sorry Darwin, It's Time for a New Excuse*

The missing links in the fossil record were clearly a very big problem for Charles Darwin and his theory of evolution. But the only explanation he could come up with was that we have "extreme imperfection" in the fossil record. In Darwin's day only a small portion of fossil-bearing strata had been investigated and so he lived in the hope that further digging would undoubtedly unearth these missing links. Since 1860 however, virtually every fossil species that has been unearthed has shown that only near-relatives of existing species ever lived. In other cases, unique species were found, unlike any we have existing today. But **never have any fossils been found that can be classified as ancestors or descendants of *other* species**. Never have *any* of the missing links, pertinent to the theory of evolution, been discovered.

87 *I Must Confess*

"...I fully agree with your comments on the lack of direct illustration of evolutionary transitions in my book.   If I knew of any, fossil or living, I would certainly have included them. You suggest that an artist should be used to visualise such transformations, but where would he get the information from? I could not, honestly, provide it, and if I were to leave it to artistic licence, would that not mislead the reader?....You say that I should at least "show a photo of the fossil from which each type of organism was derived." I will lay it on the line-there is not one such fossil for which one could make a watertight argument.....It is easy enough to make up stories of how one form gave rise to another, and to find reasons why the stages should be favoured by natural selection. But such stories are not part of science, for there is no way of putting them to the test...."[16]

88 *Factoid:*

A recent Gallup poll found that nearly half of Americans believe that God created fully developed human beings about 10,000 years ago. Another 40 percent believe the time span was millions of years, but that God directed the process. What is most surprising is that only 9% actually believe in evolution by strictly natural process. It is strange therefore that evolution is the accepted doctrine in public schools and universities.

89 *No Alternatives*

Something that the fossil record demonstrates clearly is that species appeared suddenly, with no sequential relatives. In other words, each species appears in the fossil record as if it were created then and there, with no link (or ancestor) to any older fossils. And many scientists, realizing this, are now saying that Darwin's theory that species evolved slowly over time must be incorrect. Even so, these same scientists have no idea how these species were able to evolve suddenly. Nor do they understand why. In an article dealing with this very issue, *Time* magazine noted, "Here scientists delicately slide across data-thin ice, suggesting scenarios that are based on intuition rather than solid evidence."[17]

90   *Man, the Final Creation*

After modern man appeared, no other new species appeared in the fossil record. Man appears to be the final creation. While Christians may balk at the geological dating of the fossil record, it should not be overlooked that the fossil record lines up perfectly with the *order* of creation in Genesis. Genesis tells us that **man was created last**. At the end of the sixth day, after man appeared, God rested from His creation.

91   *Punctuated Equilibrium*

Some evolutionists try to explain the sudden appearance of new species, and the fact that the links are missing, with a theory known as *punctuated equilibrium*. They suggest that when a species suffers from tremendous environmental stress and its population begins to rapidly drop off, the species then **suddenly evolves into another species**. The population of the new species then rapidly increases. There are some serious problems with this theory. For one thing, when we see a species drop rapidly in number today, it faces extinction. If the theory of punctuated equilibrium was correct, these species should mutate and grasp on to favorable new characteristics that will help them survive. Why don't they still evolve when facing extinction?

92   *It's A Miracle!*

It seems that punctuated equilibrium evolutionists would have us believe in miracles if they believe that mutations on a sudden grand scale, say from terrestrial mammal to whale, were to occur in a quick spurt. **Indeed, aren't miracles one of the major problems that evolutionists have with creationism?**

93   *Beating the Odds*

There are only a few species today that we can observe in real time, that seem to benefit from mutations. Viruses and bacteria are examples. But these creatures have populations in the quadrillions (one quadrillion is 1,000,000,000,000,000 in case you're wondering). According to theoretical calculations that were reached in the 1960s, the greater a population size, the greater the possibility it could survive mutational advancement. The reason is that **far more of the mutations in a species are harmful than favorable**. A population would have to be large enough to withstand the trials of destructive mutations until successful ones were reached, and clearly we don't see those kinds of populations in the vast majority of animal species.

94   *What's New?*

Darwin saw nature as a continuous evolutionary process following the principles of natural selection. **If the theory of evolution is correct, then shouldn't we see evidence of new**

species evolving today? In fact, we should see new species constantly appearing at a rate greater than extinction. But we don't.

95   *A Missing Link Found?*

While there are missing links in the fossil record, some species have been found that supposedly support the theory of evolution. One example is the fossil discovery of a creature known as *Archaeopteryx*, a primitive bird with some reptilian characteristics in its skeleton. But its wing was designed as are other birds, properly equipped for flight, as far as we can tell from its skeleton, Although it did have some reptilian features, this is not sufficient evidence for evolutionists to argue that the *Archaeopteryx* is indeed an intermediate step between reptiles and birds. One of the characteristics which led paleontologists to consider a link between reptiles and birds was the fact that the *Archaeopteryx* had teeth. But there are other examples of birds in the fossil record that had teeth and we also know that there are also reptiles that don't have teeth. Another characteristic present in the skeleton were claws on the wings. But ostriches have claws on their wings and they are classified as birds, not an intermediate between a reptile and a bird. Clearly, skeletal features alone are not enough to determine whether a species is part of a sequence that will ultimately lead to a brand new species.

Clearly, if evolution were indeed true, then evolutionists wouldn't have to settle for such a poor example to demonstrate their theory.

96 *What Came First, The Archaeopteryx or the Egg?*

Interestingly, a fossil has been unearthed in Colorado of a bird, that scientists claim is older, or at least as old as Archaeopteryx (see "A Missing Link Found?"). So, we know that birds *already existed* at the time when the supposed *ancestor* of birds appeared.

97 *Evolutionists Have No Guts*

One of the severe limitations of the fossil records is that they hold no real information about the soft anatomy' (i.e. internal organs) of a species. Therefore, any data about the soft anatomy would have to be based on speculation. And judging a species to be an *intermediate species* based on skeletal features alone has proven fallible. For example, for close to a century, the rhipidistian (ancient lobe finned fishes) were believed to be a suitable amphibian ancestor. They were classified as an intermediate between fish and terrestrial vertebrates because of a number of skeletal characteristics which were similar to early representatives of amphibians.

At the same time, several assumptions were made about the rhipidistian anatomy. Then in 1893, a fisherman caught a living relative of the rhipidistian in the Indian Ocean. This relative, the coelacanth, was thought to be extinct. Studies conducted on the coelacanth's anatomy showed no evidence that its internal organs were pre-adapted for a terrestrial environment. Thus, even though the fossil records may show a small handful (and much more would be needed to prove the theory of evolution) of possible extinct intermediates, experience has shown that classification based on skeletal features, without information about the soft anatomy, has proven fallible and unreliable.

98 *No Transitional Animals... But I do Have An Uncle I'm Not Sure About*

The fossil record is not the only place that scientists search for possible "intermediate species". There are animal species, living today, which some believe to be possible intermediates, or *missing links*. In other words, they are somewhere in between one species and another. The lungfish for example, has gills, intestines and fins just like any other fish. But it also has lungs, a heart, and a larval stage which are clearly amphibian. This is not proof, however, that the lungfish is an intermediate between a fish and an amphibian. The gills, for example, are not somewhere in between the two species. They fully belong to the fish species. And the lungs are fully amphibian, nothing less. Another example that is given of an existing intermediate species is the duckbill platypus. It lays eggs like a reptile, but it has many mammalian features as well. But these features are distinct to mammals, or to reptiles. They do not represent anything transitional between the two species.

Geological Columns and Fossil Dating

We know that the fossil record has played a key role in the development of the theory of evolution. But how exactly does one go about dating fossils? Georges Cuvier, the founder of modern paleontology, was in Paris when it was being rebuilt after the French Revolution. He noticed that the rock beneath the streets was layered, and that each layer appeared to contain different fossils. Later, during the Industrial Revolution, Charles Lyell and a couple of friends picked up where Cuvier left off, and developed a theory that life started out simply and then diversified into more complicated creatures (Charles Darwin, it should be noted, was still a boy at this time). They theorized that the fossils of the simple creatures, therefore, would be found in the bottom layer, and that fossils of more complicated creatures would be found in the upper layers. They set out to try to prove their theory, analyzing the layers and naming them based upon the fossils found within each. Eventually, Lyell came up with twelve Earth ages and the model he developed came to be known as the *geological column*. Today, it is upon this column that the dating of fossils is based. However, the entire rock column, created in theory by Lyell, cannot be found anywhere and there have been cases of the various layers appearing in different order, depending upon where you're digging. As it turns out, the geological column used for dating the fossil record, worked well in theory, but not so well in the cold, hard light of reality.

How Old is that Rock?

An interesting catch-22 situation exists when it comes to the methods used by paleontologists to determine the age of rocks. Since some rocks cannot be dated by the carbon-14 or radioisotope methods, scientists instead date them based on the fossils found in them. So, **basically, the paleontologist would have to look at the fossil in a rock and compare it to a similar fossil found in a textbook containing the fossil record, which in turn is based on the geological column, which is, as we've just pointed out, faulty to begin with**. So if the fossil is of a clam that the textbook fossil record claims existed about 320 million years ago, the scientist would date the rock in which the clam fossil is found at 320 million years or so, with no way to independently confirm the date.

Circular Logic is Logically Circular

Scientists are frequently called upon to calculate the age of a rock that contains no fossil record whatsoever. They do this by determining the age of the layer of rock below or above it which does contain fossils. In other words, the age of a fossil is determined by the rock strata, or its place in the geological column. And the age of the rock is determined by the fossils found in it. That's like saying a boy must be 10 because he's in grade 5, and we know he must be in grade five, because he's 10. This is circular reasoning based on theories and faulty assumptions.

102   *Evidence for an Underwater Earth*

Is there evidence that some great flood as described in the book of Genesis, actually took place? Many of the rocks that lie beneath our feet are known as sedimentary rocks. This means they were originally laid down under water, and when the water eventually disappeared, the sediment dried, hardened, and became rock. About 85% of the rock surface around the world is made up of sedimentary rock, indicating that at some time in the past, the world was covered by water.

103   *Go Fish*

Did you know that marine fossils have been discovered even on the highest mountain peaks? It's a fact. But many people say "Those mountains weren't necessarily mountains when they were covered by water. Tectonic plates have been upheaved and lowered many times through history." True. But geology *does* provide evidence as we shall see, for massive flooding in every part of the world. And the evidence seems to indicate that although these Tectonic plates had collided to form mountains, they were still above what is now sea level when these marine fossils developed. This means there must have been a major flood, significant enough to have covered these Tectonic plates.

104 *One Big Flood*

Some scientists argue that it was not one flood that engulfed the Earth, but a series of localized floods. For example, Georges Cuvier, the father of paleontology, was also responsible for the Multiple Catastrophe Theory. He believed that the banks of the Seine River overflowed several times, creating twenty-eight layers of sedimentary rock with fossils. But it was discovered later that these same layers of sedimentary rock could also be found throughout England, Germany, and even Russia. Clearly one river could not have been responsible for all of this.

Another layer or rock, known as the "chalk strata", containing marine fossils was found extending from northern Ireland, through England, to France, southern Germany, northern India, Malaysia and ending up in Australia. Indeed, this same strata extends around three-quarters of the world! Again, something more than a localized flood from the Seine, or any other river, was responsible for this.

105 *Of Course the Clams are on the Bottom!*

There is a considerable body of evidence suggesting that the various layers of rock, which supposedly contain fossils dividing the Earth into twelve ages, could have all been laid down at the same time! In 1893 geologist Johannas Vulther observed that the order of marine fossils found in rock layers often coincided with the order of their natural marine environment. So clams which live on the bottom of the ocean were often found at the bottom layers of strata. **This is exactly what we would expect in the case of a flood**. Sediments, carried by rivers and streams, would be dumped on the ocean floor, burying those creatures which lived on the ocean floor first.

106 *How did Plants Survive Noah's Flood?*

If, as the Bible tells us, the entire Earth was covered with water during Noah's flood, how did plants manage to survive. Well, a scientist named George Howe set out to solve this problem by conducting a series of experiments where he tested the ability of plant seeds to survive underwater. Seeds from various fruits and flowers were submerged in either salt or fresh water for up to 140 days. His findings demonstrated that the majority of seeds treated in such a way still managed to germinate and grow after the water was removed. The fossil record shows many examples of plants that lived in the past, but cannot be found today. This is consistent with Howe's finding that some of the plants were indeed unable to live through the hardship of a flood, while many others were just fine.

107 *Sedimental Journey*

Gilbert Hall, a sedimentologist, later picked up on Vulther's studies, and conducted several experiments using various colored sediments being

carried by a water flow. Here is what he found...
First, the heavy sediments dropped to the bottom,
while the lighter sediments were carried further by
the current. But then he noted that the heavy
sediments on the bottom actually began to progress
forward in the current, covering up some of the
lighter sediments. Eventually, he found that in
certain places, the lighter sediments actually ended
up on the bottom. We should stress here that this is
not theory. It is empirical evidence provided by
repeated experimentation. Hall proved that
sediments drop in a certain order, trapping creatures
living in their own environmental habitats, which later
became fossils. While Lyell's geological column was
simply based on preconceived biases, **Hall's
experiments prove that the sedimentary layers
in the geological column could very well have
been laid down simultaneously in a short period
of time,** rather than sequentially by a series of floods
over twelve Earth ages spanning millions of years.

108 Facts Consistent with a World-Wide Flood

Gilbert Halls' findings are consistent with
what we would expect if the flood described in
Genesis did actually take place. After the first few
days, the entire Earth would not yet have been
covered with water. But, there would have been
enough turbulent waters running from rivers and
across the land surface to rapidly deposit sediments
into the oceans. So the first thing to be buried by
these sediments would have been marine life. As
more of the Earth was covered, reptiles, amphibians
and mammals would have been destroyed and some

of them would have been buried by sediments. This is exactly what we see in the geological column. Evolutionists interpret the column as the evolutionary order of life, when indeed it could be the natural outcome of a catastrophic global flood. The bottom line: These creatures weren't necessarily buried in accordance with time periods as evolutionists suggest.

109 *Grand Canyon Cuts Deep into Evolutionary Theory*

Besides Gilbert Hall's experiments, there is further evidence found in nature itself that suggests the conventional method of dating rocks can be wrong. This in turn could suggest that proponents of a *young Earth theory* are indeed correct. Let's look at the Grand Canyon for example. This geological wonder is made up of clearly stratified layers, with the lines between them appearing to be very precise in many cases. It is thought that the Hermit shale, for example, was laid down about 10 million years before the Coconino sandstone layer which lies on top of it. Yet **the Hermit shale shows no signs of erosion**. Over 10 million years there must surely have been some erosion which would show up clearly before the next Coconino layer came about. Not all layers of the Grand Canyon exhibit this same "knife-edge" contact, but there certainly are enough to argue against a long passage of time between the layers as evolutionists claim.

Of Worms and Clams

Following Hurricane Carla in 1961, a large layer of sediment was deposited on the Texas shoreline and even out into the Gulf of Mexico. A couple of decades later, it was observed that there had been a lot of evidence of biological activity within these sediments. Plants had grown roots in the sedimentary layer and various creatures, including clams and worms, had burrowed their way down into it. In fact, within just a few years, this *bioturbation* changed the original sedimentary structure. Yet, when you look at the sedimentary layers of rock around the world, there is no evidence of such bioturbation. This seems surprising, especially when we consider the fact that these sedimentary layers were supposed to have been there for millions of years before the next sedimentary layer covered them over.

Facts Point to Creation, But Scientists Still Struggle for Alternatives

Researchers are agreed that the Earth *did* suffer mass extinction that almost caused life to be wiped out completely. It is known as "The Great Dying." There is less agreement however on what is believed to have caused it. Suggestions include volcanic eruptions, comets, greenhouse warming, and ice age cooling. **Whatever the cause, scientists tell us that it wiped out about 95% of marine life and about 70% of land-dwelling vertebrates**. Coral reefs and forests were destroyed as well.

Was the Ark Big Enough?

While speaking of the flood, let's take a look at the ark that the Bible says God gave Noah the blueprints for. The ark was massive. The Bible says it was three hundred cubits (450 feet) long, fifty cubits (75 feet) wide, and thirty cubits (45 feet) high. Naval architects made up a scale model of the ark and determined that it would certainly be large enough to hold a pair of each kind of animal, bird and insect we have today, as well as Noah and his family, and a vast food supply.

Noah's Ark: A Miracle in Itself

We have to make sure that we take an important fact into consideration when we talk about Noah's Ark. At that time, nothing of this magnitude had ever been built before! No one had the knowledge or expertise to design such a structure. Even the Roman ships of 50 BC and naval vessels during the time of Admiral Nelson were nothing in comparison to this magnificent ark. **So where did Noah get the knowledge to build such a structure that even modern naval architects have determined is absolutely suited to survive a flood of vast proportions?** That certainly gives the skeptics something to think about. In fact, even today, ocean liners use the same basic dimensions as Noah's ark.

Tree Rings Refute Old Earth Hypothesis

In 1975 John D. Morris, Ph.D., of the Institute for Creation Research suggested that the tree rings from trees in different layers of the fossilized forest at Specimen Creek be compared. It is well-known that many trees develop one tree ring per year and that this is how the age of trees can be calculated. It is also known that atmospheric conditions can leave characteristics in the tree rings. For example, an extremely wet year causes a tree to produce a wider ring. A tree that suffered from disease or insect infestation will have an abnormal ring for that year. Frost damage can also be detected through tree rings. If the fossilized trees in the various layers had grown at different times there would be no correlation in their tree rings. Dr. Morris commissioned Dr. Mike Arct to research the fossilized trees at Specimen Creek. Arct observed that the characteristic ring patterns of fossilized trees from various layers did indeed correspond. This means that the trees, even though they *appear* to have grown at different times, did in fact grow at the same time.

115

A Fossilized Forest in 15 Years?

Yellowstone National Park contains an interesting set of fossils in what is known as a *fossil forest*. For years, evolutionists have used such fossil forests as evidence of an old Earth. It appears as if layers of forest were fossilized on top of each other. At Specimen Ridge there are twenty-seven layers. At Specimen Creek there are about fifty. It would appear to require lengthy periods of time for each forest to grow to maturity, be destroyed, another forest to grow to maturity, be destroyed and so on. Some of the petrified trees in the various layers contain up to 400 tree rings. The whole sequence is assumed to take a minimum of thousands of years. But **observations of events that have taken place following the volcanic eruption of Mount St. Helen in 1980 may explain the fossilized forest in a much, much shorter time span**. During the volcanic eruption, a whole forest was ripped off the side of the volcano along with vast amounts of soil. About a million fir trees were stripped right down to the stump and landed in Spirit Lake. Over time, these trees began to get water logged and sank to the bottom of Spirit Lake. The heavier end of the tapered logs sank first in many cases. What we've ended up observing, is that many of the logs actually sunk to the bottom vertically. At the same time, different layers of sediment were laid down along with volcanic ash, which in some instances contained calcium oxide, thereby forming a type of cement. Other layers have been created from decaying tree bark which formed peat. So what we have at the bottom of Spirit Lake is layers of vertical and horizontal logs, and layers of soil, volcanic ash and peat, making it look like the fossilized forests of Yellowstone National Park. Most importantly, the results of the Mount St. Helen disaster have taken about fifteen years, not a 'minimum' of thousands.

16   *Turning Wood Into Stone*

It is important to note that it does not take
millions of years for petrified wood to form. Under
the right conditions, as discovered in lab experiments,
wood can be petrified (turned to stone) quite rapidly.
It is thought that the best conditions are for ground
water to boil through hot volcanic ash which is
replete with silica. In one experiment a piece of
wood was dropped into the silica-rich alkaline hot
water spring at Yellowstone Park. One year later,
when the piece of wood was retrieved from the
spring, it was observed that a substantial amount of
petrifaction had taken place. Indeed, petrified wood
is being produced commercially today for hard-wood
flooring!

17   **Kettles Burn Old** *Earth Supporters*

Something that is frequently seen in coal
mines is a feature known as a "kettle", which
appears as a circular rock in the roof of the mine.
What it is in fact, is the bottom of a fossilized tree
trunk that extends through different layers of rock in
the mine. So what does this have to do with the age
of the Earth? Well, the answer lies in the way that
coal is believed to have formed. It is thought that
several layers of peat accumulated over the years
and were eventually submerged beneath the ocean
and covered by sediments. The peat is then thought
to have turned into coal as a result of great heat and
pressure from being buried beneath the great weight

of the ocean waters and sediments. We know today that mud accumulates on the bottom of the ocean at about one millimeter to one inch per year. At this rate, it would require millions and millions of years for peat to become coal. And what has this got to do with the fossil trees found in coal mines? Well, if we know that coal comes from peat which has been submerged beneath the ocean, that would mean these fossilized trees, which are growing through different layers of rock and coal, would have to have been growing in the ocean over millions of years. It is well known that trees cannot survive very long in salt water—In fact, they decay in a couple of decades at the most. Clearly, this poses a major problem for the theory of evolution.

118 *Rock Layers Must Have Been Laid Down Quickly*

Fossils that extend through many strata are known as "polystrate" fossils. Not only have tree trunks been observed in different strata, but so have smaller plant life as well. Fossilized reed-like plants known as Calamites have been observed in strata of limestone in Oklahoma. The reeds are obviously more fragile than a tree and surely would not have survived the many years it supposedly took for each of these layers of limestone to be laid down. It would seem, therefore, that these layers of limestone were not laid down gradually while the reed continued to grow. Instead it seems that these layers of sedimentary rock were deposited much more rapidly by water.

119   *Global Stories Suggest Global Flood*

      Undoubtedly there have been many disasters here on Earth over the history of recorded time. Earthquakes, hurricanes, volcanic eruptions, tornados, fires, drought and disease are just a few of the possibilities that come to mind. But very few stories and legends passed down through generations within cultures talk about any such disasters, with the exception of one — a great flood. Even more amazing, is the geographical dispersion of the cultures sharing this story. From the southern tip of Africa, to the Australian outback, and from the ancient Greeks to the Babylonians, **legends of a great flood that wiped out all life except for a few humans who escaped in a boat exist across the globe.**
This suggests a common historical experience among these diverse people and nations.

120   *And You Thought Modern Men Were Pigs!*

      A lot of people refuse to believe the Biblical account of Genesis because they have been taught that man evolved from apes to man-like creatures known as hominids, and eventually to modern man. The Bible, they say, makes no mention of these cave men, and so simply cannot be accurate. While there *appears* to be archaeological evidence for the existence of such hominids, **all of the examples used to prove their existence have been either fraudulent or based on insufficient evidence.**

Take the case of the so-called *Nebraska Man* for example. In 1922 one molar tooth was unearthed in the state of Nebraska. Professor Henry Osborn, who was the head of the American Museum of Natural History, claimed that it belonged to an early hominid. An artist's depiction, *based on one tooth*, of this supposed ape man was drawn up. Later, in 1928 it was discovered that the tooth had actually come from an extinct pig. But **somehow, and this is the important point, the artist's depiction lives on!**

121   *No Bones About It*

Let's now consider the case of "Lucy." In the mid-1970s paleontologist Carl Johanson unearthed, in Ethiopia, part of a skeleton that they dubbed "Lucy". She was supposedly an early representative of a primate lineage that was bi-pedal (walked upright on two feet). Later we were told that, in reality, only 40% of Lucy's skeleton was ever found. Furthermore, Johanson later revealed in a question and answer period for an audience at the University of Missouri that **the knee joint from which he determined Lucy was bi-pedal was discovered in a rock layer that was not only 200 feet below the rest of Lucy's skeleton, it was over half a mile away too!**

122 Genesis Did Not Attempt to List Every Creature on Earth

Anthropologists claim that while some examples of the primate lineage have proven to be false, there are still enough legitimate cases to prove the existence of hominids (non-human primates that walked upright). After all, there are bones on exhibit in museums which seem to prove their existence. This is a gray area for which neither the record of nature, nor the Bible, offers a concrete resolution. But it doesn't necessarily mean that because the Bible does not mention such primates, God didn't create them. After all, the Bible doesn't mention insects in the creation account in Genesis either. Indeed, the Bible does not (nor does it claim to) give a complete and definitive account of the creation chronology. It is a highly abbreviated summary. Therefore, it is natural that entire categories of creatures such as the insect have been omitted.

123 Well I'll Be a Monkey's Nephew....Not!

Even if hominids *did* exist as anthropologists claim, there is no evidence that they were ancestors of man. What makes man distinct from other primates, and from other species? According to the Bible, God personally created Adam and Eve. He gave them a spirit. This is what distinguishes man from other living creatures. In this we are unique. Now, secular anthropologists have lumped all primate species into the same category as man. For one, they claim that the hominids used tools, so this makes them a good candidate for ancestral man. But there are some creatures today that use tools. Sea otters, for example, can be seen floating on their backs on the surface of the water with a rock resting on their stomach. They then pound sea urchins against the rock to open them up and eat what is inside. Anthropologists also claim that the hominids buried their dead. Elephants have a form of burial for their dead. When the matriarchal elephant dies the others gather around her and cover her with straw. **So the use of tools and burial of the dead are not attributes of spirit which *is* unique to man**.

124 *That's the Spirit*

What criterion could be used to distinguish spiritual man from primates? Well, the appearance of religious relics could be used. Depending on which Hebrew scholar you listen to, man was created anywhere between 6,000 to 50,000 years ago. Scientific evidence of a spiritual man, determined by the oldest known religious relic, is anywhere from 8,000 to 24,000 years ago. Therefore, the biblical dates and anthropological dates for spiritual man are not in as great a conflict as many believe.

125 *Molecular Evidence*

If the primates, including man, are all in the same family tree, there should be some biological evidence for this. However, molecular biology has demonstrated that by comparing the protein molecule sequences of the primates (monkeys, apes, man) there is no overlapping in the system of classes. In other words, **there is no evidence at the molecular biological level that any of them are relatives or descendants of one another**.

126 *The Search for Eve*

Sticking with molecular biology, evidence has been discovered which suggests that all humans came from a common human ancestor. The DNA within the nucleus of our cells contains genes which we've inherited from both our mother and our father. Recently, an interesting discovery was made regarding DNA. Mitochondria were found to exist within what are known as "power generating stations", within the cell, but outside the nucleus. The mitochondria also contain genes. But these genes are only passed on from the female. Vincent Sarich and Allan Wilson, two biochemists, were interested in doing a chart on the migration of people from around the world. They wanted to go back in time and find the women who had passed on these mitochrondrial DNA. They took a cross-section sampling of the DNA from women around the world. **They concluded from their research that the DNA characteristics of all the women they had tested came from the same woman.**

127 *A Common Ancestor?*

According to the May 26, 1995 issue of *Science,* a study was conducted on a part of the male sex chromosome in 38 men. A surprising lack of genetic variation was discovered, leading to the conclusion that modern man could indeed have come from a common ancestor.

128 *Gaps in Genesis?*

Some have used Biblical genealogies to determine the date of man's creation. When the ages from the genealogies of Genesis in chapters 5 and 10 are tallied, it takes us back to about 4,000 BC. This would mean man's creation took place about 6,000 years ago. However, archaeologists appear to have provided evidence that modern man existed 10,000 years ago. There is a possible solution to this discrepancy. **There is good reason to believe that there are some genealogical gaps in the book of Genesis**. We do know for certain that there is a gap in the genealogy of Matthew 1. Matthew 1:8 tells us that "Joram begat Uzziah," but when compared to I Chronicles 3:11-14 we are told that the genealogy went from Joram to Ahaziah, to Joash, to Amaziah, to Uzziah (Azariah). Also, we know of at least one seeming gap in the Genesis genealogy. Luke 3:36 tells us that between Arphaxad and Shelah there was Cainan. However, Cainan does not make an appearance in the genealogy of Genesis 10. Since we know there appear to be gaps in the genealogies, tallying the age of the human race by adding up the age of these genealogies is not a completely accurate method.

129 *A Bride for Cain*

We cannot close this section without addressing a classic criticism of God's creation of Adam and Eve. If Adam and Eve had only two sons, Cain and Abel (who was later killed by Cain), how could Cain get married. Well Genesis 5:4 says that in

Adam's 930 years of life he sired sons and *daughters*. Obviously Cain could have married a daughter or a niece.

130 *Did Cain Commit Incest?*

It has been argued by some that since Cain must have married his own sister, he must have therefore committed incest, which the Bible condemns. And incest results in genetic defects, as is well known today. First, the law against incest was not recorded by Moses (Leviticus 18) until hundreds of years after the life of Cain. Secondly, there were no genetic defects in the early days of the human race. Adam was created perfectly by God.

131 *Why Are There No Dinosaurs in the Bible?*

As was the case with "cave men",many people today refuse to believe that the Bible is an accurate historical record because it fails to make mention of dinosaurs. Again, we'd have to remember that **the Bible doesn't mention insects either**. The creation account in Genesis was only a summary and so the fact that dinosaurs are not mentioned does not seem to be a strong enough argument to prove that the Bible is not accurate. Indeed, not all Christians dispute the existence of dinosaurs which seems to make sense since museums across the country and around the world are filled with the remains of these creatures.

Some Christians believe that dinosaurs *are* mentioned in the Bible. While it is not a direct, literal reference, there is a reference to creatures that *could have been* dinosaurs. We have to keep in mind that the word "dinosaur" itself is only about 150 years old, so we certainly can't expect to find it in the Bible. In the book of Job, chapters 40 and 41, we find references to the *behemoth* and the *leviathan* which were two extremely large creatures which terrified man. The *behemoth,* we're told was a very large creature that ate grass, could hide in the shade of a large tree, or be covered by the willows of a brook. While there are some Christians who believe that this creature was merely a hippopotamus or an elephant, there are a couple of other descriptions of the *behemoth* in Job 40 that suggest it was something much larger. Considering that the book of Job is well known for its accuracy with regard to the laws of nature, and that the Bible itself is not prone to exaggerations as in religious myths (we will discuss these points in the next section), it seems possible that the *behemoth* was not a mere elephant or hippopotamus. Job 40:23 says for example that , "he drinketh up a river, and hasteth not: he trusteth that he can draw up Jordan [the river] into his mouth." Only a very large creature could have inspired such a description. Also, Job 40:17 describes the creature's tail like this: "He moveth his tail like a cedar." Of course we know that cedar trees are very large, and certainly the tail of an elephant or a hippopotamus could not possibly be compared to a tree. So maybe the Bible did tell us about dinosaurs, but not everyone has recognized it.

133 *God and Relativity*

In reality, a close examination of the Bible reveals many accurate scientific observations that were written long before modern scientists ever discovered them. In the early part of the twentieth century, for example , it was determined through Albert Einstein's theory of general relativity, that **the universe had a beginning, and some entity, therefore, must have been responsible for its beginning**. By definition then, this entity would have had to exist outside of the universe in order to create it. Hebrews 11:3 tells us the universe was "framed by the word of God."

134 *God Came Before Time...*

Einstein's theory of general relativity had been applied to mass and energy, hence he came up with the famous equation $E=mc^2$ (E refers to Energy, and M to Mass). In the late 1960s and early 1970s three British astrophysicists, Stephen Hawking, George Ellis, and Roger Penrose, decided to apply the theory to space and time. But what was lacking at that time was overwhelming proof that the universe was indeed governed as suggested in Einstein's theory. Scientists were only able to confirm it to 1% precision. Then a NASA rocket equipped with advanced precision technology was able to confirm to within one one thousandth of a percent that the universe did indeed conform to Einstein's theory of general relativity. **With this confirmation, it was also concluded that not only did mass and energy in the universe have a**

beginning, but time did as well. So it can also be concluded that the entity responsible for the creation of the universe not only exists outside the universe, *but outside of time as well*. II Timothy 1:9 and Titus 1:2 tell us that the promises we now have in Christ were provided *"before the beginning of time."*

135 ...And Space

The same conclusion was reached about space. What does the Bible have to say about God's existence outside of space? After Jesus (who the Bible tells us *is* God who came to Earth in a human body) was resurrected, He went to meet with His disciples in the upper room. The door was locked and He simply passed through the physical barrier. To prove He was not a spirit, but a body of flesh and bones, He invited the disciples to touch Him. He also ate fish and bread with them to demonstrate that He was indeed physical. In our four dimensional world, with one dimension in time and three dimensions in space, it is impossible for physical objects to pass through physical barriers like doors and walls. This is proof that God is not limited to our dimensions of space. So again, science has discovered what the Bible already told us.

136 *Bible Holds Only Creation Explanation That Doesn't Conflict With the Facts*

There are literally hundreds of creation stories that have come from various world religions. For example, a Chinese creation myth claims that a star canopy covers a square Earth with China at its center. The Egyptians claimed that a goddess with a starry body was resting her hands and feet on the four corners of a rectangular Earth. A Germanic legend claims a land of cold was separated by a wide valley of mist from a land of fire. A god was produced from the mist, and when the god died, all life grew from its corpse. The Mesopotamians believed the Earth floats on water. A dome covers the Earth and rain seeps through holes in the dome, while the stars shine inside the dome. The problem with each of these myths though, is that they obviously do not line up with the established facts of nature. Compared to other creation explanations from world religions, the Biblical account of Genesis is the only one which does not conflict with modern scientific evidence.

137   *Bible Years Ahead of Modern Science*

The Bible was written at a time when many religious myths were suggesting explanations for creation which we now know to be complete nonsense in light of modern scientific discovery. Many people of that day believed for example, that earthquakes were caused by the huge waves that crashed into the shore when a tortoise swam in the sea!   Many also believed that a Greek god supported the Earth with the strength of his arms. But clearly, the Bible did not partake in the popular culture of its day and God's Word, when it makes reference to the natural world, is consistently found to line up with the established facts of nature. The book of Job makes many references to the workings of the natural world. Job 26:7, for example, says, "He stretcheth out the north over the empty place, and hangeth the Earth upon it." Verse 8 says, "He bindeth up the waters in his thick clouds; and the cloud is not rent under them." So the first verse is telling us that the Earth hangs in space, and the second verse is giving us a description of evaporation.

138 — So Much for the Flat Earth Society

The book of Isaiah was written long before man discovered that the Earth was not flat. And yet we read in chapter 40, verse 22 that God "is he that sitteth upon the circle of the Earth."

139 — The Clock is Ticking.....

We know today, from the Second Law of Thermodynamics that the contents that make up the universe are running down and that the universe, therefore, is not eternal. **This was big news to modern science, but not the Bible**. In fact, centuries before scientists even thought of the idea, the Bible made it very clear. In Psalm 102:25 and 26, we are told that the universe, created by God, is going to wear out like old clothing. Isaiah 34:4 tells us that the "host of heaven shall be dissolved, and the heavens shall be rolled together as a scroll: and all their host shall fall down."

140   The Earth is "Not Made Up of Things Which Do Appear"

One of the most astonishing scientific references in the Bible talks about atoms which cannot be seen. In fact, the Bible tells us that the "worlds were framed by the word of God, so that **things which *are seen* were *not* made of things which do** appear." (Hebrews 11:3) But most people don't know that there must be the right number of protons, neutrons and electrons in the universe in order for life to exist. For example, neutrons are (and must be) 0.138% more massive than protons. A change of even one tenth of one percent either way, and life would be impossible.

141   Hygienic Laws of God Proven by Modern Medicine

Many of the hygienic laws that God gave to the Israelites have also been proven by modern medicine to be accurate. When the black plague struck Europe and when leprosy spread, the Jews in many instances were blamed because these plagues weren't running rampant in the Jewish ghettos. Why? Because they didn't have sewage running in their streets as was the case in many other cities, like Paris, for example. There, sewage was running into the Seine River and people were not only bathing in their own filth, but drinking from it too! . We can still see this kind of thing taking place today in countries like India and Egypt which are not Christian nations and therefore do not follow the principles of the Bible. **By following the hygienic laws of the**

Bible, the Jews throughout the ages have managed to avoid many of the plagues and diseases that have stricken other cultures.

142 Dietary Tips Directly from God

In addition to the hygienic laws that God gave to the Israelites, he also gave them many commands regarding their diet. They were instructed, for example, not to eat meat like pork, which we know today needs to be cooked with extreme care since it carries parasites. They were instructed not to eat fish without scales like lobster or crab, which are suspected today of containing cancer causing agents. They were also instructed not to eat meat and dairy products together which we now know to be very hard on the digestive system. So these dietary laws were not merely for religious reasons, as many believe, but they were also given for health reasons — and sound advice it was!

143 God's Wisdom in the Operating Room

Now let's consider the Jewish custom of circumcision in which the flesh of the male foreskin is cut off. The Israelites were instructed to perform circumcision on the eighth day after birth. Only in recent years has it been discovered that **the blood clotting factor in a baby doesn't reach its maximum peak until the eighth day after birth and then it drops down again!** So, according to modern science, the eighth day is the ideal time to perform circumcision. So important was this instruction in fact, that the rite was not postponed even if the eighth day was the Sabbath.

144 *The Case for Circumcision*

Interestingly, many doctors and hospitals today will perform circumcisions upon request because it is known medically that men who have not been circumcised are more likely to cause cervical cancer in their wives. There is a very low rate of cervical cancer in Jewish women.

145 *The Birth of the Sanitation Industry*

The book of Deuteronomy (23:13) says that the Jewish soldiers were to have a "paddle", or a shovel, attached to their weapons so that when they had to "ease" themselves they could dig a latrine and bury it. Up until World War I, about ten times as many soldiers died of disease as they did from war wounds because they did not know enough to dig a latrine and bury the human waste. The book of Deuteronomy was written by Moses who had been educated by the Egyptians. They believed, for example, that wounds could be healed by rubbing them with dung from a camel. **How did Moses discover that burying waste was more hygienic than using it for medicinal purposes?** Another wonderful proof of God's divine hand guiding the writings of the Bible.

Bible Recognizes Role of Germs in Disease

In the late 1800's, Louis Pasteur developed his theory that germs cause disease, not poisons which develop in the organs as other scientists believed. Also predominant in that day were many myths, in a number of cultures, suggesting that evil spirits were the cause of disease. **The books of Leviticus and Deuteronomy, however, written hundreds of years before, are filled with various hygienic references on how to keep disease at bay**. If someone was sick, the Israelites were instructed to cover any open vessels that contained food or beverages. If someone was suffering from a plague, the Jews were instructed to remove them outside the camp, with someone being designated to go with them and take care of them. They were instructed to constantly cleanse their hands and clothing while treating patients. Some Viennese bishops who followed these rules during a plague in the 1600s managed to stop the plague cold. So the Bible obviously recognized that disease was caused by the spreading of germs—years before scientific discovery could catch up!

Christian Doctor Applies Biblical Teaching and Saves Lives

A Christian Quaker by the name of Joseph Lister picked up on Pasteur's work and became the founder of antiseptic surgery. He worked on several experiments that would lead to the practice of disinfecting surgical tools. Even so, it still it took a very long time for hospitals to adopt the practice of complete hygienics. In many hospitals across Europe in the early 1900s, for example, doctors would leave an autopsy room and then go and deliver a baby without washing their hands in between. Needless to say there was a great mortality rate for both birth mothers and newborns while this practice was going on. Later, one Christian doctor decided to implement some of the things he learned from the Bible and had the staff in his hospital department start washing their hands in between each medical procedure. The result? A dramatic reduction in the mortality rate within his department! Indeed, it took many years for scientists to discover' that germs even existed, and that they could be passed through the air or from unsanitary medical procedures.

148 | *Biblical References to King Herod Verified by Recent Finds*

For many years skeptics have worked very hard trying to find fault with the Bible. But through their incredible efforts, they have only managed to establish stronger and stronger evidence proving just the opposite—that the Bible is in fact, totally accurate. **Some of the best evidence for Biblical accuracy comes from the field of archaeology where modern day research has unearthed solid evidence for the people, places and events mentioned in the Bible**. The Bible talks for example about a King named Herod. Recent archaeological digs have proven beyond the shadow of a doubt that such a king did in fact exist, and lived

right where and when the Bible says he did. For
years historical scholars doubted that Herod even
existed, but now coins bearing Herod's name have
been unearthed proving that the Bible was right.
Archaeological digs at Samaria, Caesarea,
Jerusalem, Jericho and Masada all have uncovered
items proving the existence of this king.

149 *No Contradictory Evidence Ever Found*

Other characters and places in the Bible are
also known to have existed through evidence
provided by archaeology. For example,
archaeologists have unearthed the remains of King
Solomon's palace and of the stables at Megiddo. The
pool of Bethesda in Jerusalem, described in the Bible
has also been uncovered. Indeed, the land of Israel
contains an abundance of historical treasures, and
every single one of them, supports the Biblical
account of history.

150 *Physical Proof for the Existence of King David*

Another historical figure whose very
existence was questioned was the Biblical King
David, for whom there appeared to be no real
physical evidence. However, in 1993 at Tel Dan in
Israel, a piece of rock was discovered that actually
bore the inscription "House of David" and "King of
Israel." Time Magazine summarized the discovery
like this: "This writing—dated to the 9th century BC,

only a century after David's reign—described a victory by a neighboring King over the Israelites. Some minimalists tried to argue that the inscription might have been misread, but most experts believe Biran and Nivah [the two archaeologists who discovered the chunk of basalt at Tel Dan] got it right. **The skeptics' claim that King David never existed is now hard to defend**."[18] This proof of David's existence is especially important since Jesus Christ, if He is the Messiah (we will study this in a later section), was prophetically required to be a descendant of King David.

151   *Evidence for the Existence of Jesus Christ*

One of the most important historical questions of course is the question of whether or not Jesus Christ ever actually existed. Well, archaeologists have discovered 1st century artifacts which bear His name, proving at least that someone of that name existed and lived around the time the Bible says that Christ lived. Furthermore, the fact that modern time has been recorded with reference to BC and AD seems to suggest the existence of a prominent person by this name. The Jewish historian Josephus, who was not a believer in the divinity of Jesus Christ, makes mention of Him, as well as His brother James. In *Antiquities* he wrote, "But the younger Ananus who, as we said, received the high priesthood, was of a bold disposition and exceptionally daring; he followed the party of the Sadducees, who are severe in judgment above all the Jews, as we have already shown. As therefore

Ananus was of such a disposition, he thought he had now good opportunity, as Festus was now dead, and Albinus was still on the road; so he assembled a council of judges, and brought before it the brother of Jesus the so-called Christ, whose name was James, together with some others, and having accused them as law-breakers, he delivered them over to be stoned." **So it seems clear, historically at least, that Jesus Christ did exist and lived in Israel just as the Bible teaches.**

152 — *Pontius Pilate Says "Hey, That's My Seat!"*

Another prominent Bible figure whose existence was doubted by many historians due to lack of archaeological evidence, was Pontius Pilate. However, one of the greatest Roman historians, Cornelius Tacitus, makes mention of him in his *Annals* (xv. 44) (AD 54-68). Writing of the account of Nero's persecution of Christians, Tacitus recorded, "Therefore, to scotch the rumor [that Nero had instigated the fire which ravaged Rome in AD 64], Nero substituted as culprits, and punished with the utmost refinements of cruelty, styled Christians. Christus, from whom they got their name, had been executed by sentence of the procurator Pilate when Tiberius was emperor." Furthermore, during archaeological digs at a Roman theater in Caesarea, Israel, a stone that had been used as one of the theater seats was overturned. The inscription on the stone, which had originally been used as a road sign, bears the name of Pontius Pilate.

153 *Jericho Finding Backs Biblical Chronology*

Research conducted by British archaeologist Kathleen Kenyon confirmed the existence of a place described in the Bible as Jericho. However, her investigations lead her to conclude that Jericho could not have existed after 1550 BC, clearly contradicting the Biblical chronology of its destruction by Joshua and the Israelites. Years later however, other archaeologists found evidence that showed Kenyon's date was incorrect and that Jericho's existence did indeed fit with the Bible's chronology.

154 *Joshua's Report Verified*

According to a paper published by the *Biblical Archaeology Review* (March/April 1990), remains from the city of Jericho clearly show that its demise did indeed line up with the Biblical account . The evidence shows that the city was strongly fortified; that it was attacked after the spring harvest; that there was not enough time for the inhabitants of Jericho to flee with food supplies; that the siege did not take long enough for the city dwellers to use up their food supply; that the walls were leveled in a manner that provided easy access for the siege to take place; that the invaders did not loot the city; and that the city was indeed burned after the walls were leveled. **Each of these findings lines up perfectly with the account given in Joshua 2 and 6.**[19]

155 Let the Bricks Fall Where They May

During excavations in the early 1930s, it was determined from the remains of the walls of Jericho that the walls were not pushed inward as one would expect, had they been knocked down by attackers with battering rams. Instead, the walls seem to have fallen straight down, as if the Earth had disappeared beneath them. The Biblical account tells us that they were knocked down supernaturally.

156 I'm Still Standing

When the walls of Jericho fell, they fell straight down, consistent with what one might expect during an earthquake. But there is something else unusual about the way they fell. It seems that almost all of the walls fell, with the exeption of a portion of the northern wall. There, the wall somehow managed to remain standing. The Bible tells the story of Rahab, a Canaanite prostitute who hid the Israel spies who came to assess the city. She hid them in her home which was built against the city wall. She was told to bring her family into her house and that they would be spared. The Bible tells us that Rahab's house was somehow spared when the rest of the city fell. **Archaeologists not only found that part of the wall remained standing, but that there were houses built against that portion of the wall**.

157 — The "King" That History Forgot

Daniel 5 tells us that Belshazzar was the king of Babylon during its demise. However, archaeologists could never find proof for the existence of such a person. In fact, the evidence pointed to Nabonidus as king of Babylon at that time. However, Daniel's account as recorded in the Bible has been confirmed by more recent archaeological discoveries. Nabonidus was indeed king of Babylon from 556 to 539 BC. But in 553 BC he left on a long journey, leaving his first-born son, Belshazzar, in charge. So when Cyrus overthrew Babylon, Nabonidus was in northern Arabia and Belshazzar was the reigning king. This fact was discovered when archaeologists unearthed a document known as the "Persian Verse Account of Nabonidus." Before this document, Belshazzar was unknown since Greek historians were mainly interested in official kings. Because Belshazzar was only a subordinate, his name was not recorded as the reigning king and historians soon forgot about him completely.

158 — No Trespassing!

In the book of Acts, we are told that the apostle Paul had started a riot in Jerusalem when he took a group of Gentiles into the Jewish temple. While Gentiles *were* allowed in the outer court of the temple, they were not permitted to go beyond this area. The Jews even put up signs in Latin and Greek warning that any Gentile that went beyond the outer court would face death. In 1871, one of these Greek notices was discovered in Jerusalem confirming the Biblical account. The notice left little room for misinterpretation and said simply "No foreigner may enter within the barricade which surrounds the temple and enclosure. Anyone who is caught doing so will have himself to thank for his ensuing death."

159 *"The Church of God is an Anvil That Has Worn Out Many Hammers"*

The archaeological proofs for the accuracy of the Bible also demonstrate its historical accuracy. **The Bible has been criticized more than any other book in the world, and yet it has withstood the tests of time and the constant assaults by its critics.** H.L. Hastings once said, "Infidels for eighteen hundred years have been refuting and overthrowing this book, and yet it stands today as solid as a rock. Its circulation increases, and it is more loved and cherished and read today than ever before. Infidels, with all their assaults, make about as much impression on this book as a man with a tack hammer would on the Pyramids of Egypt." When the French monarch proposed the persecution of the Christians in his dominion, an old statesman and warrior said to him, "Sire, the Church of God is an anvil that has worn out many hammers.' So the hammers of infidels have been picking away at this book for ages, but the hammers are worn out, and the anvil still endures. If this book had not been the book of God, men would have destroyed it long ago. Emperors and popes, kings and priests, princes and rulers have all tried their hand at it; they die and the book still lives."[20]

160 *Bible A Survivor*

Not only has the Bible withstood the test of time from its verbal critics, it has also withstood the test of time from those who have tried to *physically* eradicate it. In 303 AD, for example, Diocletian commanded that the Bible be destroyed. But, says Bernard Ramm, "The Bible has withstood vicious attacks of its enemies as no other book. Many have tried to burn it, ban it and outlaw it from the days of Roman emperors to present-day Communist-dominated countries.'"[21]

161 *Biblical "Internet" Discovered*

Something that had, until recent years, hindered historians from verifying many of the historical records of the Bible was the fact that they could not understand many of the ancient languages found on ancient artifacts. In 1822 a Frenchman by the name of Jean Champollion unlocked what was known as the "tongue of Pharaoh". This allowed historians to finally be able to read a wealth of Egyptian writings. Later, a similar achievement was made by a British army officer named Henry C. Rawlinson. His research added three more ancient languages to the list of languages we could now understand. These new translations were then used to decipher the writings on some clay tablets found at Tell el-Armana in Egypt. Contained on the tablets were official communications between Egypt's Pharaoh and the rulers of Babylon, as well as

governs of Palestine, Phoenicia, Syria, and some
lesser Asiatic nations. This discovery proved, as had
been suggested in the Bible, that the **nations in this
part of the world were all able to communicate
with one another, and with the mighty empire of
Babylon, with great ease.**

162 *How Do You Run from Denver to Colorado?*

Sir William Ramsay, one of the most famous
archaeologists to have ever lived, devoted intense
study to the gospel of Luke. Ramsay doubted the
authenticity of Luke because of what seemed to be
historical discrepancies within the book. One such
apparent discrepancy was Luke's account that Paul
and Barnabas fled from Iconium to cities in the
province of Lyconium (Acts 14). Historians however,
were in agreement that Iconium was in fact a city,
located in the province of Lycaonia. This would be
like saying that they fled from Denver to Colorado.
So it was determined that whoever wrote the gospel
of Luke, must not have been familiar with the
geography of the area. Ramsay's research however,
and other archaeological discoveries revealed the
fact that during the time Paul and Barnabas had fled
from Iconium, the city was part of the province of
Phyrgia, not Lycaonia as historians had previously
believed. Once again, the Biblical account was
correct.

163 *Census Practice Confirmed*

Another supposed inconsistency in Luke's gospel was his reference to the fact that Joseph and Mary had to return to Bethlehem, which was the city of Joseph's lineage, to pay taxes (Luke 2:1-3). Historians did not believe that any such decree had ever actually been given. However, during an archaeological dig in Egypt, a copy of a Roman edict dated at 104 AD was unearthed. That edict, given by C. Vibius Maximus, Roman prefect of Egypt, stated, "The enrollment by household being at hand, it is necessary to notify all who for any cause soever are outside of their administrative districts that they return at once to their homes to carry out the customary enrollment..." This document therefore confirmed that such decrees which obligated citizens to return to their places of origin for administrative purposes did indeed take place.

164 *Luke's Chronology Right After All*

The verification of census procedures led to another apparent inconsistency. Luke referred to a census that took place under the reign of Caesar Augustus. Historians claimed such a decree would actually have taken place in 6 or 7 AD, making Luke's timing incorrect. But historians are now in wide agreement that there was indeed a census at the time Luke suggested. These types of censuses took place every 14 years, and according to the investigations of Ramsay (*Was Christ Born in Bethlehem?*, 1898), the papers that recorded these censuses noted that there was one which took place in 8 or 7 BC. Now this census did not just apply to Israel (the Romans referred to it as Palestine). It applied to all of the territory held by Rome. And because such a registration would take several years to complete, it is likely that it did not take place in Israel until later than 8 or 7 BC. This would fit perfectly with Luke's chronology.

165   *Right Again!*

Other criticisms of the gospel of Luke included his reference to Philippi as a "district" of Macedonia. The Greek word for district is *meris*. Historians believed the author of the gospel of Luke had used the word incorrectly. However, archaeological discoveries later demonstrated that the word *meris* was indeed used for district.

166   *Word Game*

Another word that the author of Luke was accused of misusing was *duumuirs*, representing a Philippian ruler. Once again it was later determined that Luke was correct. There were other words as well, such as *praetor*, *proconsul*, and *politarchs*, that Luke had used correctly, despite the doubts of historians.

167 *Historian Switches Sides*

Luke also stated (2:2) that Quirinius [Cyrenius] was governor of Syria at the time the census was to have taken place. Historians contended that it was *Saturninus* who was governor of Syria at the time because Israel was under the authority of the Roman governor of Syria. However, an inscription found at Tiber revealed that Quirinius had been governor not once, but twice, first between 10 and 7 BC and later in 6 AD. So, once again, **Ramsay's investigations into the seeming historical inaccuracies in the gospel of Luke confirmed that Luke was indeed correct**. So amazed was Ramsay at what he found, that **even though he had initially set out to prove that the Bible was historically inaccurate, he eventually became a believer** and a popular apologist for the New Testament.

168 *Table of Nations Amazing Even Today*

Albright was also amazed, as other historians later came to be, at the accuracy of the "Table of Nations" listed in Genesis 10. Albright noted that it "remains an astonishingly accurate document...[and] shows such remarkably modern' understanding of the ethnic and linguistic situation in the modern world, in spite of all its complexity, that scholars never fail to be impressed with the author's knowledge of the subject."[22]

169   *Did Moses Write That?*

Critics who adhered to the belief that Moses could not have written the first five books of the Bible, the Pentateuch, claimed that writing simply did not exist at the time of Moses. However, in 1964 the first of what have become known as the Ebla tablets was unearthed at the site of Tell Mardikh in northern Syria. These tablets contain writings on law codes, judicial procedures and case law. Because the Ebla tablets are about one thousand years older than the Mosaic law, we know that the written word had already been developed at the time Moses would have written the Pentateuch.

170   *Culture More Advanced Than Many Believe*

Other discoveries have also been made which prove that writing was already significantly established at the time of Moses. Josh McDowell reported, "Cyrus Gordon, formerly professor of Near Eastern Studies and chairman of the Department of Mediterranean Studies at Brandeis University and an authority on the tablets discovered at Ugarit, concludes similarly: the **excavations at Ugarit have revealed a high material and literary culture in Canaan prior to the emergence of the Hebrews.** Prose and poetry were already fully developed. The educational system was so advanced that *dictionaries in four languages* were compiled for the use of scribes, and the individual words were listed in their Ugaritic, Babylonian, Sumerian, and

Hurrian equivalents. The beginnings of Israel are rooted in a highly cultural Canaan where the contributions of several talented peoples (including the Mesopotamians, Egyptians, and branches of the Indo-Europeans) had converged and blended. The notion that early Israelite religion and society were primitive is completely false. Canaan in the days of the Patriarchs was the hub of a great international culture.'"[23]

 ## *Did You See That?*

Perhaps the greatest evidence for the historical accuracy of the New Testament however is the fact that there were so **many eye witnesses** to the events recorded there. The apostles, in their preaching, noted that they were witnesses to the resurrection of Jesus (Acts 2:32). They also said they knew that some in their audiences were witnesses to the testimony of Jesus Christ as well. In Acts 2:22 they are recorded as saying, "Men of Israel, listen to these words: Jesus the Nazarene, a man attested to you by God with miracles and wonders and signs which God performed through Him in your midst, just as you yourselves know." And those who recorded the Bible took great care in ensuring that what they were saying was true. Luke for instance (1:1-3) noted, "Inasmuch as many have undertaken to compile an account of the things accomplished among us, just as those who from the beginning were eyewitnesses and servants of the Word have handed them down to us, it seemed fitting for me as well, having investigated everything carefully from the beginning, to write it out for you in consecutive order, most excellent Theophilus." If the recorders of events had misrepresented history, or had made errors in their recordings, surely there would have been enough people to come forward to dispute these errors and set them right. **If someone wrote a book today saying that John F. Kennedy was killed by a bow and an arrow, there are still many witnesses around who would step forward and set the record straight.**

172 *Hostile Witnesses*

It must be remembered that many of the witnesses to the New Testament events were hostile witnesses who would certainly not have put up with any inaccuracies, especially if they served to prolong a religion they despised.

173 *That's the Gospel Truth*

Conclusions about Biblical accuracy can be drawn by comparing the four gospels of Matthew, Mark, Luke and John. A very simple study reveals that all four gospels, especially the first three, have a great amount of information in common. Yet their writing styles are totally different clearly demonstrating that they were each written by different people. But, because the details and evidence given in their testimonies conform to each other so closely, it attests to their accuracy. On this note, it is interesting that each of these men gave a consistent picture of Jesus Christ as the Messiah, the Son of God.

174 *That's Quite an Achievement*

It's not only the four gospels in the New Testament that show such remarkable unity. The entire Bible is completely consistent, an incredible feat considering the fact that it was **written over a span of about 1,400 years by a diverse group of people** from various lands, *with no meaningful contradictions*.

175 *Still the Same*

When considering the accuracy of the New Testament, one should take into account the "rumor" game. In this game one person whispers something into the ear of another person, who then whispers the message into the ear of someone else, and so on. Anyone who has played the game knows that by the time the message gets back to the originator of the message, it is completely altered. Almost two thousand years have passed since the time Jesus was on Earth, and until Johann Gutenberg invented the printing press in 1450, the Bible was hand copied, and new hand copies were made from other copies. One would think that through all these duplications, the Bible we read today would be completely different from the original record of events. Unfortunately, there are no original manuscripts known today of the New Testament. The oldest fragment of the New Testament is known as the John Rylands manuscript, and it is dated at 130 AD. There are however much more substantial manuscripts in existence which date back to around 300 AD. And there are thousands of other early manuscripts, in full or in part, in existence. Through tireless comparisons of the various available records, Bible scholars have been able to conclude that while there are some minor differences, such as the word "and" or "the" being added or left out, there have been no errors found that change the actual doctrine of the New Testament.

Hey, That's Not Fair

Other ancient writings, from which we base much of our history today, have very few existing copies through which we can study their accuracy. For example, there are several manuscripts of Caesar's *Gaelic Wars*, but only about ten of these are of any use. If historians are willing to accept the historical accuracy of this ancient writing, and others, with so few manuscripts available for verification, they should also be willing to accept the historical accuracy of the New Testament, especially when thousands of copies are available to study and compare that do not conflict with one another.

New Testament Most Current

The oldest substantial copy in existence of the New Testament dates to somewhere around 300 AD. This is only about 200 years after the New Testament was completed in the latter part of the first century. **There is no other historical document of this age available today which was recorded, or re-recorded, so close in time to the actual occurrence of those events.** To cite Caesar's *Gaelic Wars* as an example once again, the oldest available copy of it was written about 900 years after the life of Caesar. Another example would be Sophocles' plays. The oldest useful copy of this work was written about 1400 years after Sophlocles died.

178 Old Testament Documents Consistent with New

The Bible has been translated into many languages over the years. In fact, it has been **translated into more languages than any other book in the world!** Surely it would not be unreasonable to expect there to be a lot of translational errors made in the process. The oldest available translations of the Bible, in Latin and Syriac, are dated at 150 AD. This was, of course, in the second century, one century after the New Testament was completed in the original Greek. Studying the translations however, **researchers did not uncover any significant variations** which would change the doctrine of the New Testament.

179 My Kingdom for a Xerox Machine!

Now that we've looked at the New Testament, let's shift our focus slightly and ask the obvious question: What about the Old Testament? Since it dates back in history to about 4,000 years before Christ, it is argued that there must be a lot of historical errors in it. Because of its age, there are not as many early manuscripts of the Old Testament available as there are for the New Testament. And there are no copies available which were recorded as soon after the occurrence of the original events as there are for the New Testament. However, this is not a reason to dispute the Old Testament's accuracy, as one might expect. Indeed, the Jews took great care in ensuring that each new copy of the Old Testament was recorded without error. The Jews took painstaking care in ensuring that each new copy made of Biblical books was recorded carefully and without errors. They had intricate systems set up for cross-checking their work, and when they had completed a new copy they were so convinced of its accuracy, they gave it equal authority to older copies. So confident were they in fact, that once the new copies were completed, they often burned their old copies which had become worn out with use.

180 *Could the Old Be Newer Than the New?*

Some have stated that the Old Testament prophetic books, such as Isaiah, were actually written *after* the events themselves took place. In about 700 BC Isaiah prophesied that Cyrus would declare that Jerusalem was to be rebuilt and the foundation of the temple was to be laid (44:28). Remember, at the time Isaiah wrote this, the temple of Solomon was standing and Jerusalem was already a bustling city. How then could Isaiah have known that the Babylonians would destroy Jerusalem, level the temple, and that someone named Cyrus would give the order that their temple and Jerusalem be rebuilt? Either Isaiah was shown the future, or this book of the Old Testament was altered later to fit the events that took place in the future. It was difficult to prove the latter was not the case before the discovery of the Dead Sea Scrolls in the caves at Qumran in 1947. The Dead Sea Scrolls consist of about 40,000 inscribed fragments, from which scholars were able to put together 500 biblical books. Most importantly, their **studies of the scrolls proved conclusively that Isaiah, (and other books of the prophets), were not altered at later dates to fit the actual events.**

181 *An Eye for Detail*

Amazingly, careful study of the Dead Sea copy of the book of Isaiah, dated at 125 BC, showed that all the words in this document **matched virtually word for word** with a document of Isaiah dated at 980 AD, thus demonstrating once again the accuracy with which the Jews had recorded new copies over a period of a thousand years.

182 *Old Prophecies Legitimate*

Other ancient manuscripts have been discovered that further confirm the authenticity of the Old Testament. In the hills near Wadi Muraba'at, for example, a parchment dating from 700 BC has been found. Parts of leather scrolls have also been found containing portions of Genesis, Exodus and Deuteronomy. The various manuscripts pre-date the beginnings of Christianity and have **provided Bible scholars with the certainty that Old Testament prophecies, and prophecies dealing with the Messiah, were not altered after the events themselves had taken place.**

183　　　*No Time for Stories*

　　While the historical accuracy of the Bible
has been proven time and again, critics still have
trouble with some parts of the Bible that appear to be
nothing more than myth. Take, for example, the story
of Jonah and the big fish. Jonah's prophetic account
is given in the biblical book that bears his name. The
historical account of the same story is given in II
Kings 14. Jesus, in Matthew 12, told the Pharisees
that they would be given a sign that He was the
Messiah, just as they had demanded. He compared
his death, burial and resurrection to the story of
Jonah being in the belly of a big fish for three days.
If Jesus knew that the story of Jonah was a fable,
why would He compare it to the historical fact of His
own death and resurrection? By comparing His
death and resurrection, which are the foundation
stone of Christianity, to a myth, He would not be
providing any support for His prophetic claims of
Messiahship.

184　*Right From the Fish's Mouth*

　　Physical evidence has now been found to
support the existence of Jonah. For one, his tomb
has been found in Northern Israel. Also, ancient
coins have been found that bear the image of a man
coming out of a fish's mouth.

185　　*The Miracle of Miracles*

　　Many people have difficulty accepting some
of the stories in the Bible, especially those requiring

miracles. But based on the trustworthiness of the Bible in the areas of geography, history and science, one should be willing to give the miracle accounts some serious consideration as well. The gospels of course, center on the life of Jesus Christ. The authors of the gospels were all agreed that He was the Messiah, the Son of God. Because of His Deity, it is ridiculous to try to understand His many miracles through our understanding of modern science. By their very nature, miracles are above natural laws (or they wouldn't be miracles, would they?). If Jesus is truly a divine being, we really would naturally expect Him to be able to manifest His divine power through the performance of miracles.

186 Any Way You Look At It, Jesus Was Real

It may come as a surprise to some people that not all accounts of, and evidence for, the miracles performed by Jesus come from Christian sources. The Jewish historian Josephus for example made mention of Jesus' miraculous deeds in *Antiquities* (xviii. 3. 3.). He notes, "And there arose about this time Jesus, a wise man, *if indeed we should call him a man*; for he was a doer of marvelous deeds, a teacher of men who received the truth with pleasure. He led away many Jews, and also many of the Greeks. *This man was the Christ.* And when Pilate had condemned him to the cross on his impeachment by the chief men among us, those who had loved him at first did not cease; *for he appeared to them on the third day alive again, the divine prophets have spoken these and thousands of other wonderful things about him*: and even now the tribe of Christians, so named after him, has not yet died out." Some scholars suggest that the italicized sections were added later by Christians who had transmitted Josephus' text, not the Jews. Nonetheless, the remaining text does verify the historical existence of Jesus and His "marvelous deeds."

187 *Early Writings Confirm Historical Jesus*

When Jerusalem was destroyed in 70 AD, the supreme court of the Sanhedrin fell along with it. In order to keep Jewish spirituality alive, a group of Pharisees compiled a religious code known as the Mishnah. Over the years several commentaries, the Gemaras, were developed around the Mishnah. Together they are known as the Talmud. There is little reference to Christianity in the Talmud and what we do find is nothing short of hostile. But according to the commentaries of earlier rabbis, there did exist a Jesus of Nazareth who was described as a transgressor in Israel because, among other things, he practiced magic. For his transgressions he was executed on Passover Eve. So again, we find **non-Christian historical sources verifying the fact that Jesus did indeed perform miracles**, even though these sources ascribe them to sorcery.

188   *Could the Resurrection Have Been a Hoax?*

The greatest miracle accounted for in the Bible is that of the resurrection of Jesus Christ. Indeed, it is this miraculous event that forms the very foundation of Christianity. Over the years many have tried to explain away the resurrection. One theory that has been suggested for the empty tomb following Christ's resurrection is the possibility that Jewish or Roman authorities actually removed the body themselves. This suggestion only raises the question, "Why?" And if they did, why did they not come forward and reveal what they had done, bringing forth witnesses to the fact? And why did they not present the corpse to prove they had it? After all, it was Christ's resurrection that was the foundation for this new sect that the Jewish and Roman authorities would have preferred to stamp out of existence. **If they had proof that the resurrection was a hoax, surely they would have come forward.**

189   *Jesus Says "No" To Drugs*

Others have tried to explain away the resurrection by suggesting that Jesus took a drug which made Him appear to be dead when in fact He was still very much alive. Later, He was revived, giving the appearance that He had been resurrected. But according to Matthew 27:34 Jesus even refused to take a drug that was commonly given before crucifixion to help numb the pain, so this suggestion seems highly unlikely.

190 | *Was The Cross Deadly?*

There is also strong evidence to refute
claims that Jesus did not actually die on the cross. By
its very nature, crucifixion was designed to ensure
the death of the prisoner. Jesus was also beaten
severely prior to the crucifixion and was in fact so
exhausted from the beating that He was unable to
carry the cross Himself. The nails that were pierced
through His hands (actually the wrist area) and feet
would certainly have pierced nerves, causing
excruciating pain and severe blood loss. But
ultimately, death by crucifixion was death by
suffocation. The victim had to try to hold up his body
in order to breathe. All the weight of the body would
be placed on the arms which would surely have been
dislocated by the force. Jesus was on the cross from
morning until sunset. Surely such torture would result
in the death of even the most physically fit person.

191 | *Just Making Sure...*

How did the centurion determine that Jesus
was dead? The Bible tells us that he thrust a spear
into Jesus' side and blood and water came out. The
water was likely fluid that had either built up
between the membrane and wall of the heart, or
between the lung and the wall of the chest cavity, or
both. But when this water came out, the centurion
knew Jesus was dead.

192 *Deadly Force*

Medical authorities who have examined the account of Jesus' death claim He would have to have died on the cross. Take for example this quote from the *Journal of the American Medical Society* (March 21, 1986): "Clearly the weight of historical and medical evidence indicates that Jesus was dead before the wound to his side was inflicted and supports the traditional view that the spear, thrust between his right rib, probably perforated not only the right lung but also the pericardium and heart and thereby ensured his death. Accordingly, **interpretations based on the assumption that Jesus did not die on the cross appear to be at odds with modern medical knowledge**." (p. 1463)[24]

193 *Another Confirmation*

Joseph of Arimathea, a follower of Jesus, requested Jesus' body after the crucifixion so that he could bury it in his tomb. Pilate re-confirmed that Jesus was dead prior to releasing it to Joseph. And you can be sure that Pilate wanted to be certain that this trouble-maker' was gone for good.

194 *The Impossible Robbery*

Some try to explain away the resurrection by claiming that the disciples stole the body of Jesus from the tomb. However, there were safeguards in place to protect against just such a possibility. For one thing, there were Roman guards posted at the tomb around the clock, to make sure nothing happened to the body. Also there was a Roman seal put on the tomb. The Roman guards knew if they fell asleep, giving the disciples an opportunity to steal the body, they would be put to death. Obviously under those circumstances, the guards would have pretty good motivation to stay awake and make sure they kept their eyes on that tomb. And **even if they had been foolish enough to fall asleep on the job, it would be hard to imagine them sleeping right through the tremendous noise of a giant stone being rolled away from the door of the tomb.** There was also the fact that the grave clothes that had been wrapped around Christ's body, and the napkin which covered his head, were left behind in an orderly fashion. This suggests that the body was not stolen. Surely grave robbers would have taken the body in the grave clothes, or at least thrown them aside haphazardly, on the floor. It's hard to imagine them, already risking their own lives, taking the time to neatly fold the clothes and leave them in a nice pile for the guards to find in the morning. It seems much more likely that they would simply cast them aside and run for their lives.

195   *Surprise!*

The fact that the disciples were so surprised to see Jesus after His resurrection strongly suggests that they were not in on a conspiracy to steal His body from the tomb. And they had never really understood the resurrection when He was trying to explain it to them during His ministry before his death.

196 *Eye-Witness News*

Another key fact to take into account is the sheer number of people who were actual eye-witnesses, who actually saw Christ after His resurrection. In I Corinthians 15:5-6 the apostle Paul said that **Christ was first seen by Peter [Cephas], then by the twelve apostles, and then by 500 brethren!** Even Paul said that some of these 500 were still alive during the time of his preaching. Surely if the resurrection had been a hoax, at least one or two of these people would have come forward and set the record straight.

197 *Seeing is Believing*

Another evidence for Christ's true identity is Saul of Tarsus, who later became known as the apostle Paul. Saul was a great rabbi, who hated and persecuted Christians. So great was his zeal against them in fact that he actually had them thrown into prison and even had many of them killed. **Who knew better than Paul what could happen to someone who became a Christian? And yet he still chose to become one himself!**
Why would Saul of Tarsus then decide to become a Christian? He gave his reason. He said that he met the resurrected Jesus Christ while on the road to Damascus. But how do we know he wasn't just having some kind of hallucination which he sincerely believed to be true? Well the Bible gives us proof. In Galatians, chapter 1 Paul tells us that he was made an apostle, not by man, but "by Jesus Christ" (verse

1). As for the teachings of Jesus Christ he said, "neither was I taught it, but by the revelation of Jesus Christ" (verse 12). Paul even tells us that when he became a Christian he didn't go to meet with the apostles in Jerusalem, but he went to Arabia and then returned to Damascus. It wasn't until three years later that he finally went to Jerusalem where he met the apostle Peter. By this time, Paul had become such an authority on the Christian gospel that he even pointed out to Peter some scriptural errors he was making (Galatians 2:14). The other Christians present had to agree that Paul was right and the apostle Paul, who learned the gospel by the revelation of Jesus Christ, went on to write most of the New Testament.

198 *From Cowards to Heroes?*

Another convincing evidence that these events were not a hoax can be found in the very actions of the disciples themselves. **These men were, when you get right down to it, doubters and cowards.** They turned and ran away from the Garden of Gethsemane when Jesus was taken captive. Peter denied his Lord three times in the face of personal danger. And yet something happened to these men that they "turned the world upside down" (Acts 17:6). They lived in poverty, suffered many trials, and all but John died cruel deaths. Peter was crucified upside down, at his own request because he did not feel worthy to die in the same manner as his Lord had. Andrew, Peter's brother, was crucified. Philip was stoned and crucified. Bartholomew was skinned alive. Thomas was killed with a spear near Madras, India. Matthew was killed during a missionary journey in Egypt. James was crucified. Jude was killed in Persia. Simon was crucified. Mathias was martyred in Ethiopia. And John, after being imprisoned on the Isle of Patmos, was released and died a natural death. **If the Bible and the accounts of Jesus Christ and His divinity were a hoax, why would these men go through what they did?** What did they have to gain?

199 *Motive?*

And what about Jesus Christ Himself? What did He have to gain? He received no great wealth or worldly possessions by concocting such a hoax about Himself. Indeed, if it was all for nothing but a lie, all He did manage to get for Himself was a horrible and early death.

Conclusion of Part 1

The creation of the universe and life on Earth were one-time events. And just how these events actually came about will never be proven by science. We have demonstrated that the creation theory should not be so readily dismissed as simple religious myth and despite what many people believe today, it has never been proven that the creation account of Genesis contradicts the scientific truths that we know today. We also feel we have provided enough evidence to prove that the popular and widely-accepted evolution theory is simply that, a theory. It is not scientific fact and yet today it is widely accepted as truth without factual proof to back it up. Indeed, there is much scientific evidence which can be used to argue against the theory of evolution and when you get right down to it, a belief in the theory of evolution would require as much faith as creationism, if not more, once the scientific evidence has been examined.

Are the universe and the Earth as old as scientists and evolutionists tell us? We have demonstrated that the conventional methods for dating the universe and the Earth are not as fool-proof as we have been led to believe. Furthermore, the possibility that the Earth is in fact very young can be supported in light of other data. Did man come from a long line of primates through random developments over many years? There is no scientific evidence to back this theory either. Most importantly, we believe we have provided sufficient evidence that the universe and life on Earth were created by a designer. **This evidence suggests that we and our universe did not just come into existence through chance accidents!**

Part 2
Startling Prophecies

Introduction

If there was an intelligent designer of this universe, as all the evidence suggests, then the implications are staggering. It means that there is someone, or something, bigger than us out there!

We've also seen how the Bible contains information that the writers could not have possibly known in the times in which they lived. So it is a remarkable book to be sure, **but is it a message from God?**

Well, if it is, you would surely think that He would have included a way that we could authenticate His message. In other words, you would think that the One who created us with keen, curious and inquisitive minds would have expected us to use those minds as we sought to verify that this was indeed a message from Him.

According to the Bible, that proof is to be found in the many prophetic passages within its pages. In fact, about one quarter of the Bible is made up of prophecy — events predicted before they happen! No other religious book in the world even attempts to foretell the future. Yet, the Bible does provide clear, detailed and amazing prophecies about the future and the end of the world as we know it. If those prophecies are indeed accurate, then there is proof positive that this book deals in a realm well beyond our understanding.

To give a sense of what we are talking about here, we would like for you take a moment to take something we call the 'prophet test'. Close your eyes for a moment and assume that our world will be here for at least 2,000 or so more years. Now try to picture what the world will be like after those two thousand years have passed!

You can't do it, can you? If you are like most people, you just draw a blank. Why? Because you have no frame of reference to even begin to imagine that world. You know it would be nothing like today, but you don't have any idea what it will be like.

Now let's reverse that for a moment. Let's imagine a guy sitting in a stone house in the Middle East 3,000 years ago. Your world would have consisted largely of sheep, stone tools and water wells. How could someone from that time and that frame of reference have possibly seen into our world.

Through all of our modern day scientific knowledge we cannot possibly explain how such a thing could be possible. And, nowhere else in the world does any book contain detailed prophecies like those of the Bible.

Remember, God says He will prove the Bible is a message from Him by the fact that He can tell us history before it happens (Isaiah 46:9-11). So, let's start with our world today. It is safe to say that there is more prophecy about the day you and I live in than in any other time in human history! So, we have an opportunity to judge the accuracy of these prophecies that span thousands of years.

Finally, there is something else that we should mention. **If these prophecies are indeed being fulfilled right before our eyes, then the message that they contain is a staggering one: We are living in the last days before the second coming of Jesus Christ to this Earth!**

Let's start with the single event that the Bible told us would mark the beginning of the last days' countdown...

200   *They're back*

The date was May 14th. The year was 1948. It had been almost nineteen centuries since the armies of Titus had flattened Jerusalem. At four o'clock that afternoon, David Ben Gurion entered the Tel Aviv Museum and made a declaration to the world: **"Today a Jewish nation is born and it's name is Israel."** It was an amazing event. But even more staggering was the fact that this day had been prophesied throughout the Old Testament. The prophet Ezekiel wrote that **"In the latter years thou shalt come into the land that is brought back from the sword, and is gathered out of many people, against the mountains of Israel, which have been always waste: but it is brought forth out of the nations...."**[25] Isaiah said much the same thing, **"And it shall come to pass in that day, that the Lord shall set his hand again the second time to recover the remnant of his people which shall be left...and shall assemble the outcast of Israel and gather together the dispersed of Judah from the four corners of the Earth."**[26]

201 *The Last Dance*

It is important to point out that **the Bible also said that when the Jews returned to their land, that event would be the sign telling us that we had entered into the final generation of history as we know it.** Ezekiel, in his vision, saw that the time frame for this regathering was in the "latter years."[27] But, it was Jesus himself who laid out the time-frame most clearly. Using the common symbolism of Israel as a fig tree, He described the time in which the re-born nation would emerge from a long winter and stretch forth her leaves. "Now learn a parable of a fig tree; When his branch is yet tender, and putteth forth leaves, ye know that summer is nigh....So likewise ye, when ye see these things begin to come to pass, know that the kingdom of God is nigh at hand."[28]

202 *Oh Jerusalem*

God not only told us that Israel would be regathered into her own land in the last days. He also specifically made it clear that after years of domination by foreign powers, Israel would once again possess Jerusalem as her capital. And, indeed, these were two separate events. **While Israel became a nation in 1948, she did not gain full control of Jerusalem until the Six Day War in 1967**. In Zechariah 12:6, God promised that "Jerusalem shall be inhabited again in her own place." Jesus Himself, foretelling the coming destruction of Jerusalem, warned, "And they shall fall by the edge of the sword, and shall be led away captive into all nations: **and Jerusalem shall be trodden down of the Gentiles, until the times of the Gentiles be fulfilled**" (Luke 21:24). As it turns out, the times of the Gentiles lasted until June of 1967!

203 *What a Waste!*

Ezekiel 38:8 says that in the last days the Jews would be gathered back into the promised land, after it had *laid waste* for many years. **In 1697 Henry Maundrell, writing of the Holy Land, said there is "nothing here but a vast and spacious ruin."** In 1738 English archaeologist Thomas Saw said it was "barrenness and scarcity." In 1785 Constantine Francois Volney used words like "ruined" and "desolate" to describe the Holy Land. In 1867 Mark Twain wrote, after his visit to "Palestine," that across the Jezreel Valley "There is not a solitary village throughout its whole extent...There are two or three small clusters of Bedouin tents, but not a single permanent habitation" (*The Innocents Abroad*). Of Galilee he said it was "unpeopled deserts" and "rusty mounds of barrenness." The same types of descriptions were given for Judea, Bethlehem and Jerusalem. And even in 1948, when Jews began to return to Israel, it was an unprosperous and unfruitful piece of desert property.

204   *The Wandering Jew*

Looking back at the history of Israel and the prophecies related to her, is one of the most staggering proofs that the God of the Bible is indeed who He says He is. After the Israelites had been freed from slavery in Egypt, God selected Moses to lead them to their promised land. But, He warned them that if they didn't obey His commandments, He would remove them from this land. He was also very specific that they would ultimately be scattered into every nation on the Earth: **"And the Lord shall scatter thee among all people from the one end of the Earth even unto the other."**[29] Did this happen? Yes it did. The Israelites did disobey God, and true to His word, He allowed them to be taken into captivity into Babylon. Ever since the Babylonian captivity, about 2,500 years ago, the Jews have been scattered about in nations all around the world. Still, in all of that time, the Jews have never lost their identity and we all know that today **the phrase, the wandering Jew,' has even become a cliché.**

205   *Scape Goats for the World*

God had also warned the Israelites on their way back from Egyptian captivity that if they disobeyed Him, He would make them "an astonishment, a proverb, and a byword, among all nations whither the Lord shall lead thee....And among these nations shalt thou find no ease, neither shall the sole of thy foot have rest: but the Lord shall give thee there a trembling heart, and failing of eyes,

---

and sorrow of mind. And thy life shall hang in doubt before thee"[30] **Perhaps no other people in history have been hated and persecuted as much as the Jews. Even today we hear rumors of so-called Jewish conspiracies to control the banking industry, the media, and the world.** The Jews have often been blamed for outbreaks of plague and disease. They were kicked out of nations many times. There were the Russian pogroms, and eviction by the Moors from Spain. They were persecuted as heretics during the Inquisition. But perhaps the greatest manifestation of this fulfilled prophecy was the Nazi holocaust during which 6 million Jews were killed for simply being Jewish. And it was at the end of the holocaust that many Jews were inspired, out of desperation for survival, to return to the land of Israel. Today, in many nations, anti-Semitism is still on the rise.

206 *Against All Odds*

Any military analyst in the world today will tell you that Israel's survival, since being re-born in 1948, is nothing less than a miracle. The prophet Ezekiel foresaw that God would indeed perform miracles to keep His re-gathered people safe. Speaking to a last-days enemy of Israel, God said, "when my people of Israel dwelleth safely, shalt thou not know it?"[31] Ezekiel foresees that "they shall dwell safely all of them."[32] When Israel became a nation in May 1948 she was immediately attacked by surrounding Arab enemies who had been heavily armed by the military might of the Soviet Union. Israel hadn't even been a nation for one full day when the first attack came. But unbelievably, Israel won, and even expanded her boundaries! **Israel went on to survive three more major attacks in following years despite being consistently outnumbered in tanks, troops, and fighter planes.** For example, in the Six Day War in 1967, the ratio of Arab artillery was five to one in the Arabs favor, planes 2.4 to one, and tanks 2.3 to one. Yet, it was Israel who won the war and recaptured East Jerusalem, the West Bank and the Golan Heights. Even to this day the Israeli military is widely respected as the finest on Earth. But, if the prophets are right, they have an unseen ally.

207 *Jerusalem: A Burdensome Stone for All People*

The prophet Zechariah prophesied that in the last days Jerusalem would become "a cup of trembling unto all the people round about" and "a burdensome stone for all people."[33] Israel has now declared its capital to be the city of Jerusalem— a united Jerusalem. However, 90% of the nations of the world still refuse to recognize Jerusalem as Israel's capital. International embassies in Israel have had to be set up in Tel Aviv. Today, one of the greatest stumbling blocks to the Middle East peace process centers around Jerusalem. The Palestinians want East Jerusalem to be the capital of a Palestinian state, but the Jews have refused to allow Jerusalem to be divided again. Today, the international community is strongly pushing Israel to allow Jerusalem to be "on the table" for the sake of the peace process. Clearly, Jerusalem is a stumbling block to peace...exactly as was prophesied.

208 *The Death and Birth of Hebrew*

About 2,000 years ago the ancient Hebrew language was lost. Even during the days of Jesus, the Jews were speaking *koine*, the common Greek language of the day. The exception was in temple worship, where Jewish priests did use about 7,000 ancient Hebrew words in their activities there. As time went on, the Jewish people spoke the language of the nations in which they had established their homes. But in our lifetime, a Jewish man by the name of **Eliazar ben Yahuda, who was living in Palestine, decided to undertake the task of reviving the Hebrew language. He restored the 7,000 words that were used in ancient Israel by the Jewish temple priests. He created new Hebrew words for modern technology like cars, planes, and computers, and today Hebrew is the national spoken language in Israel.** This achievement is a fulfillment of the prophecy uttered by Zephaniah who prophesied that God would "turn to the people a pure language, that they may all call upon the name of the Lord, to serve him with one consent."[34] Of course, most Jews today are not religious. Even so, their pure language *has been restored* for the day when they do recognize their God and will call upon His name.

209 *Temple Worship OK!*

The prophet Daniel foresaw that during the last days, at the time of the antichrist, the Jews would have reinstated temple worship. The Jews, however, have not had their temple in Jerusalem since 70 AD. Even with the recapture of the Temple Mount in 1967 the Jews have not been able to rebuild the temple because they have allowed the Arabs to maintain control of the Temple Mount. **Sitting right where the Temple would be erected are the Dome of the Rock and al-Aksa Mosque, two of the holiest sites in all of Islam.** Despite the fact that the Jews do not have a temple today, many religious Jewish organizations have been making preparations for this future temple. One group has prepared a **model** and **blueprints**. Another group, using the instructions found in the Bible, is **fashioning the precise instruments** that will be needed for temple rituals. Still another has been **training Levitical priests**. While the Temple is not yet in place, there are many groups ready to pounce on the opportunity the moment it arises.

210 *The Last Temple is Gone!*

The last Jewish temple, known as Herod's Temple, was destroyed in 70 AD by Titus and the Roman armies. These armies tore the temple down stone by stone, searching for gold that they believed was hidden between the stones. In fact, they dismantled it so completely that today archaelogists don't even know exactly where on the Temple Mount it stood. When the disciples asked Jesus about the temple He said, "...verily I say unto you. There shall not be left here one stone upon another, that shall not be thrown down."[35]

211

Land for Peace
-A Deal from Hell?

Though it has not yet been fulfilled, the Bible does prophesy that in the last days, the nation of Israel will enter into a peace agreement with a great deceiver that the Bible calls the antichrist. Of that agreement the Bible says that this leader "shall divide the land (Israel) for gain".[36] It is very interesting that **the heart of the current Middle East peace process is centered around deals that trade land for peace'.** While it has yet to be fulfilled, it is remarkable that this 2,500 year old prophecy does tell us the exact issues that would be on the table.

212

The Polar Bear

The prophet Ezekiel said that when Israel was back in her land, in the last days, she would be invaded by a confederacy of nations led by a great military power to the uttermost' north of her.[37] **If you look at a map and draw a line from Israel to the North Pole the country to the uttermost' north of her is Russia. In fact, the line almost goes through the middle of Moscow!** Today Russia is a nation in peril. Her economy is in shambles and internal strife rules the day. One thing is certain however…Her military is still one of the strongest in the world. She is major nuclear power. It is clear that Ezekiel was speaking of Russia when he spoke of a great military power that would be to Israel's uttermost north when she was regathered into her land.

213 *Surprise!*

According to the prophets, the world will be shocked when Israel is invaded by a great northern military power in the last days. According to Ezekiel, the startled nations will not even know why Russia has led such an invasion.[38] A few years ago no one would be surprised if the Russian armies moved anywhere. That was the rule of the day. They headed a global empire with fearsome armed forces. But **today, the world believes that Russia has given up her expansionist goals.** In fact, it would be safe to say that such an invasion would catch today's world totally off guard. Yet, her military might still sits there. **Her navy is four times larger than the US fleet, she has 3 times the number of submarines, ten times the number of tanks and armored personnel vehicles and twice the number of troops!**

214 *The Company She Keeps*

According to Ezekiel 38:6 this great northern power would have many allies in its invasion force.[39] By studying the genealogies of the nations listed by Ezekiel, it is a rather easy process to compare them to the modern day nations that exist today. The list includes **Russia, Turkey, Iran, Libya, and Sudan**. An international intelligence agency, based in the United Kingdom had this recent insight into the middle eastern puzzle: "It is widely assumed that **Iran** is irrevocably opposed to the Arabs negotiating peace treaties with Israel, but this is a misunderstanding of its position. Iran is happy to see

Israel forced into territorial retreat, particularly if this means returning the Golan Heights to Tehran's ally **Syria**. The terrorist campaign is not aimed at stopping the peace process, it is aimed at putting maximum pressure on Israel to compromise with Syria.... A pro-Iranian Islamist regime is already in power in **Sudan**, **Libya** is firmly in the anti-Israel camp, and Egypt and Algeria are under severe threat from Islamist rebellions. To the north and east of Israel, the position is not much better. Syria and its Lebanon protectorate are close allies of Iran...Even ostensibly pro-Western **Turkey** is moving closer to Iran in order to facilitate its economic activities in Central Asia for which Iran provides the link....The final part of the Iranian-constructed anti-Israeli coalition is **Russia**. Little has been heard of Russian activity in the Middle East since the end of the Cold War, but Iran has been very careful to nurture relations with Moscow."

215 *Russia is the Leader of the Pack!*

In describing the great invading force, the prophet Ezekiel says to this great nation to the uttermost north of Israel, "...be prepared; yes prepare yourself, you and all your companies that are assembled about you, and you be a guard and a commander for them."[40] There is no doubt, if you look at the group of nations listed in this invading force, that Russia is the military leader of the pack. But she has also supplied most of them with the military might they now possess.

216 *The Return of the Russian Jews*

We mentioned previously that God promised the Jews that in the last days He would bring them out of the nations of the world and into their own land. The prophet Jeremiah specifically said that one of the places from which the Lord would regather them would be "from the land of the north."[41] Immediately following the fall of the Iron Curtain, many Jews who had been trapped in the former Soviet Union began to leave in a mass exodus. The majority headed to the land of Israel. **To this day, Israel continues to regularly send planes into the former Soviet Union to bring back Jews who are now, for the first time in decades, free to leave.**

217 *Let My People Go*

Could it be possible that Russia's motive for attacking Israel will be her own regret over releasing the Jews. Since the mass exodus of Jews from the former Soviet Union, anti-Semitism has increased dramatically in that country. There are widespread conspiracy rumors which blame the Jews for Russia's present problems. Fueled by an extremely slow and difficult journey toward democracy and capitalism, a new outbreak of anti-Semitism has erupted there. **Extreme nationalist Vladimir Zhirinovsky summed up the mood by saying, "There is no such thing as a poor Jew in Russia...while the poorest people in Russia are Russians."** And, today, the Russian version of Adolf Hitler's "Mein Kampf" and items sporting swastikas are among the most popular sale items for peddlers in Russia.

218 *The Grass Looks Much Greener Over There*

In the spring of 1995, an explosion in one of Russia's natural-gas pipelines drew attention to the decrepit state of its more than 300,000 miles of oil pipelines. Russian government reports said there were more than 700 major leaks per year. With the spring thaw of the same year, Russians began to feel the effects of a 100,000-ton oil spill in Usinsk. The oil spill, according to a *Toronto Star* article, "contaminated an area roughly equal to 70 football fields. It includes six major streams and dozens of minor creeks...The extent of the damage from the latest Usinsk spill can only be compared with the ravaged and torched oil fields of Kuwait." As if this were not enough, the 1995 grain harvest in Russia was the worst in 30 years. **With oil spills ruining water sources for people and livestock, and with grain harvests decreasing, the mood of the have-nots is beginning to turn hateful towards, and envious of, those who do have.** Moreover, the Russian military giant is one just waiting to be awakened. Indeed, Ezekiel said that Russia would move into the Middle East "to take a spoil" of goods.[42] Today you can't deny that the need is there. Nor can you deny that the power to take what they want also seems to be there.

Shades of Alfred Hitchcock?

God says that He will destroy this northern army on behalf of Israel. In fact, He says to "Gog", "Thou shalt fall upon the mountains of Israel, thou, and all thy bands, and the people that is with thee: **I will give thee unto the ravenous birds of every sort, and to the beasts of the field to be devoured.**"[43] Interestingly, Israel is the capital of the world when it comes to the spring migration of large birds. According to a popular bird watchers' magazine, Dr. Reuven Yosef, Ph.D. and his partner went to Eilat, Israel where **they observed tens of thousands of Steppe Buzzards making their way across Israel to Europe and Asia.** Other large birds they observed were Black Kites, Ospreys and Steppe Eagles. According to Dr. Yosef (*Wildbird*; Feb. 1995), "During spring, some *two million* soaring birds traverse Israel on their way to their nesting areas...During the spring of 1994, staff and volunteers from the International Birdwatching Center in Eilat (IBCE) recorded a total of *1,022,084 raptors* comprising 29 species...Would you believe an average of *11,110 raptors were counted each day*!" A raptor is a bird of prey. Yosef continues, "The secret of enjoying raptor-watching is knowing the appropriate time and place to visit. **In my opinion, the best place in the world to see large numbers of birds of prey during spring migration is Eilat, [Israel]**..." [emphasis added]

220 *They're Dead, Jim*

One of the most incredible things about the Bible is the fact that it contains a number of staggering prophecies that could not have been fulfilled at any time in history —until now! For example, in the 24th chapter of the book of Matthew, Jesus was speaking of the time when He would return to Earth. **One thing He said was that if He didn't come back at the exact right moment "there should no flesh be saved."** How could such a prophecy have been possible at any other time in history? Certainly the power to destroy all flesh on Earth is a much more recent development. The bows and arrows, or even muskets and cannons of old could certainly not account for such a prophecy. But today this has all changed. With the development of nuclear, chemical and biological weapons, the possibility of self-annihilation is, for the first time in history, not only a possibility, but also a grave concern.

221 *From the Wright Brothers to the Space Shuttle....*

The prophet Daniel, writing from ancient Babylon over 2,500 years ago, said that one of the key distinguishing characteristics of the last days would be that "knowledge shall be increased." Of course, knowledge has increased in every generation, but what Daniel was referring to was the fact that **there would something special about the increase of knowledge in this final generation**

— the generation that saw Israel return to her land. It is pretty obvious how remarkable this prophecy is. Had you been able to travel through time — say from 75BC. to 1,300 AD — you wouldn't have seen that many dramatic changes. You could have easily adapted to the small changes that had been made. **Each generation was only slightly more knowledgeable' than the one before it. That has been true of every single generation except this one.** In just over one hundred years we have seen a rapid increase in knowledge. In 1876 Alexander Graham Bell patented the telephone. This invention revolutionized the world of communications. In 1885 Daimler and Benz developed the forerunner to today's gasoline engines. In 1903 George and Orville Wright flew the first practical airplane. In 1926 the television came into the world. In 1928 penicillin was discovered by Fleming. In 1943 the first computer was completed, paving the way to an unbelievable revolution in information technology. 1945 was the year the atomic bomb was dropped on Hiroshima. In 1957 Russia launched the first satellite into space. In 1953 the DNA molecule was mapped out. In 1969 Neil Armstrong became the first man to walk on the Moon. In 1982 genetic engineering was born, its first product being human insulin from bacteria. We have seen the advent of wireless communications, test tube babies, sophisticated weapons like "smart" bombs, and much, much more. **No other generation in human history has seen such an expansion of knowledge as ours! And today, with our accumulation of knowledge doubling every 24 months, the pace continues to increase.**

222 The "Smart" Mark

The Bible tells us that in the last days the antichrist will rule over a world economy. But the details that we are given of this economy seem to come right out of the latest sci-fi movie. The Apostle John tells us that everyone on earth will have to "receive a mark *in* their right hand, or in their foreheads: and that no man might buy or sell, save he that had the mark, or the name of the beast, or the number of his name."[44] Today, domestic pets and livestock are already having microchips implanted below their skin for easy identification in place of the old methods of branding or tattooing. Of course we haven't seen these microchips injected into people yet, but the reference in Revelation 13 suggests that such a practice may not be far away. Now consider this recent report: "...there is an identification system made by the Hughes Aircraft Company that you can't lose. It's a syringe implantable transponder....A tiny micorchip, the size of a grain of rice, is simply placed under the skin. It is so designed as to be injected simultaneously with a vaccination or alone..."[45]

223 Testing the Mark

Wired magazine, a publication on the latest computer technologies, analyzed the potential of human implants recently — "Of course the burning question is, What about people? There would be no technical problem, says Barbara Masin, director of operations for Electronic Identification Devices, in implanting the chips in humans. But to avoid a public relations nightmare, the Trovan dealer agreement specifically prohibits putting chips under the skin."[46] *Popular Science Magazine reports* "If we had our way, we'd implant a chip behind everyone's ear in the maternity ward,' says Ronald Kane, a vice president of Cubic Corp.'s automatic revenue collection group. Cubic is the leading maker of smart card systems for mass transit systems, highway tolls, parking, and other applications and one of a number of companies and government agencies pushing the frontier of smart cards—the money of the future. For Kane and his colleagues, the next best thing is giving everyone a card—a high-tech pass with a memory that may, sooner than we imagine, replace cash in our wallets."[47] The Apostle John foresaw this emerging technology, from a dusty island almost 20 centuries ago.[48]

224 *Will that Be Hand...*

Today, people have become accustomed to using PINS (or Personal Identification Numbers) in conjuction with their banking cards, security cards, cellular phones, and home security systems. But, many of these people are beginning to forget which PIN or password is for what. This is one of the reasons that the idea of biometrics is catching on in Europe and is just starting to be of interest to North Americans. **Biometrics, quite simply, are methods of identification based on a unique, personal characteristic, like a voice or a fingerprint. The most popular methods of biometric identification right now are fingerprint ID and *hand* geometry.** A letter to the editor of the *New York Times* noted, "Your report (Business Day, March 21) stated that Visa International will introduce a plastic card embedded with a microchip that can store amounts of money and be used for small purchases. ITN news has reported that such cards are used in Belgium and will soon be tried in Britain. I would like to see some charge version of the hand (or just fingerprint) scanning ID that is in the Dustin Hoffman film Outbreak'. It would be great not to have to carry any cards at all and to buy things simply by sticking one's hand briefly into a scanner. (March 21, 1995)"[49]

225 ...Or Forehead?

There has not been much progress so far in the area of biometric technology for facial recognition. But, by the mid 1990's, things began to pick up in this area as well. An article in *Popular Science* reported, **"You may never have thought of your face as thousands of points of light, but that's the way a computer sees it. New software and accessories are making it possible for computers to digitize, analyze, and identify faces."**[50]

226 Where there's a Will ...there's a Way

Compare these two statements made almost 2,000 years apart. The first was made by the Apostle John: "And he causeth all, both small and great, rich and poor, free and bond, to receive a mark *in* their right hand, or in their foreheads: and that no man might buy or sell, save he that had the mark, or the name of the beast, or the number of his name."[51] Now compare that to these words penned by by Terry Galanoy, the former director of communications for Visa International: "Protesting too loudly about it isn't going to help either, because the disturbance you kick up is going to end up in one of your files. And on that come-and-get-it day when we're all **totally and completely dependent** upon our card — **or whatever survival device might replace it** — you might be left all alone without one!"[52]

227 *The Technology Exists*

The Apostle John foresaw a worldwide system where no one would be able to slip through the cracks'. He said that no one, anywhere on Earth, would be able to conduct any kind of transaction whatsoever unless they received this mark.[53] How could this have been achieved in an any other generation before this one? Even today, with all of our modern technology, a person can still go into a corner store and buy a choclate bar, without anyone ever having to know about it. But, imagine if cash was outlawed and you could only use your credit card. And then imagine that your credit card number was cancelled? Sound far fetched? One plan to eliminate cash in favor of computerized, theft-proof smart cards claims that "it would bust up oganized crime, put an end to the deadly traffic in illegal drugs, reduce espionage and terrorism [and] drastically curtail corruption and tax evasion..." With such powerful examples clearly demonstrating the advantages of eliminating cash, there is widespread agreement that it's only a matter of time. So now in the same generation that saw Israel return to her land, we have both the technology to electronically record every transaction *and* the motivation to use it!

228   *Let me Pull up your File*

If, as the Apostle John forsaw, there was a system that would allow every financial transaction on Earth to be tracked, you would also need to be able to track the people making those transactions. Bob Gellman, for 18 years the counsel to the Congressional subcommittee dealing with these issues says that most Americans have no idea how far we've come. He says that "this is all just invisible to people and they have no idea that pieces of their lives lie scattered in these different files....What is going on slowly is that there are more and more links being created between these records. We are getting closer and closer to the notion of some kind of centralized dossier on people. We are not there yet. But that is where we are headed."[54] The Deputy Director of the Center for Democracy and Technology, JanLori Goldman, warns that "there is information that is created about you, that is created in databases, stored in databases, all over the world, and will be maintained there. You can store information electronically for a very, very, very long time. It is cheap. It is easy. So you essentially create an electronic web of information that is like a dossier, that is like a biography, pieces of information that are all over that can be pulled together essentially with the push of a button."[55]

The Book of Revelation also tells us that the antichrist will cause "all" people to take this mark. If they don't, they will simply be cut out of the economy, unable to carry out any financial activities whatsoever. In fact, it says in Revelation 13 that "no man" will be able to buy or sell anything unless he accepts the mark. The summer of 1995 saw the release of a Sandra Bullock movie, called **"The Net"**. In that movie, Bullock found herself completely locked out of the economic world, the victim of a few strokes on a computer keyboard. The story revealed that the conspirators had hacked' their way into critical government databases and completely changed Bullock's identity. They also managed to steal her passport, identification and credit cards, and because she was a loner with no friends or family, and because she worked in her own home where she had no interaction with the outside world, she found herself with no way of proving her true identity. A special screening of the movie was given to a VIP audience of executives from corporations like the Rand Corp. and the US Justice Department's computer crimes division. According to a *Toronto Star* report, **the audience "emerged from the screening impressed but unsettled by what they had seen. They told us everything in the story was accurate and plausible—frighteningly so,'** reports the movie's director, Irvin Winkler."

230 — The "Mother of all Speeches"

The Bible describes the rise of the antichrist onto the last-days world scene in powerful terms in the 13th chapter of the book of Revelation. That chapter speaks of a great world leader rising onto a global stage and winning the hearts of "all the world". But how, in any other generation, could anyone become the favorite man on the planet? How could any man even make himself known to the rest of the planet? **But, today ask Michael Jackson, O.J. Simpson or even Tonya Harding how hard it is to become one of the most famous people on the planet.** Through the advent of modern communications technologies and television it is now possible for one man to truly speak to the whole world. Just ask Ted Turner.

231 — The Image of the Beast

The 13th chapter of the book of Revelation tells us that the antichrist's partner, the false prophet, is going to make an _image_ of the antichrist ("the beast") for the world to worship. The false prophet, we are told, will have the **"power to give life unto the image of the beast, that the image of the beast should both speak, and cause that as many as would not worship the image of the beast should be killed."** Imagine a first century prophet trying to describe **an image that comes to life**. It could have made no sense to him. Yet he wrote it down. Today, we are just beginning to discover the incredible wonder of holograms. **A**

hologram is simply a three-dimensional image, made only of light, that can be made to look so much like a real object that you actually think you can reach out to touch it - but alas, there's nothing there. Even more amazing is the fact that these holographic objects can easily be manipulated to make them appear to be moving, or even speaking. Clear 3-D images that can be seen in daylight, without special glasses, were created in the mid-90s by a New York company using optics and computer programming. So real are these images in fact, that a number of department stores have taken an interest in the technology to display their products. A holographic figure could be created for example, to model clothing sold in the store.

232 *Mr. Data Gone Bad*

A real look at the prophecy of the Image of the Beast would not be complete without considering the great strides that have been made in recent years in the field of robotics. According to an article in the *Amarillo Daily News*, "A robot named Cog—inspired in part by Commander Data of Star Trek: The Next Generation'—may become a humanoid that will interact with regular folks."[56] **A product of artificial intelligence, Cog is using its brain to learn how to see just like a human baby would.** Cog's creator Rodney Brooks, a professor of electrical engineering and computer science at MIT says that Cog will have to reach the level of a two year old child to be considered a success. Now, whether or not any of these existing technologies will actually be used to create the image of the beast is, of course, impossible to say. But it is certainly interesting to note that no other generation in history had the technology to even make such a prophecy seem feasible. Perhaps we should end this point with the final words of Time Magazine's cover story on **artificial intelligence** in their March 25th, 1996 issue. They concluded with the words of computer theorist Tom Ray, **"We need to be prepared for an intelligence that is very different from our own."**

233   *We are the World*

     The key defining characteristic of the last days world foreseen by the prophets was the birth of the first truly global society. This new world order would unite mankind religiously, economically, militarily and politically. At the heart of this order stands a world government, and according to the Apostle John, this government will rule over "over all kindreds, and tongues, and nations". Daniel saw it as a system that would ultimately "devour the whole Earth."

     Such a system has never existed. But today, with the advent of instant global communications, global travel, global television and the resulting global economy, there is a growing consensus that our increasingly interconnected world does require a global government. The man who may have set this whole thing in motion with his Perestroika — or New Thinking, was Mikhail Gorbachev. Acclaimed as a visionary, he folded the Soviet Union with the purpose of joining a world community. As he put it, "this world is one whole, we are all passengers aboard one ship, the Earth, and we must not allow it to be wrecked. There will be no second Noah's Ark"

     By the fall of 1995, Gorbachev had moved to

the world stage. At his "State of the World Forum" in San Francisco he brought together 500 heads of state, spiritual leaders, scientists, corporate heads and intellectuals to explain to them how nationalist loyalties needed to be replaced by global consciousness. From there, Gorbachev toured the US with former heads of state George Bush, Margaret Thatcher and Brian Mulroney to advise business and intellectual elitists on their role in the transformation.

Pope John Paul II has also suggested that the UN be made something more than simply a political entity, that it "become a moral center where all the nations of the world feel at home." There seems to be amazing consensus in this vision of a UN that oversees world affairs ranging from the fair distribution of ocean or natural resources, to global policing, to a world court that could effectively bring international criminals to justice. While the prophesied world government has not yet emerged, the fact is that **we do now have the most powerful leaders on Earth committing their total efforts toward building a united world order**. And, it is all happening in exactly the same generation that saw Israel come back into her land. Just as the Bible prophesied!

234 *World Religion*

The Bible tells us that at the heart of this new world order there would be a new worldwide religion. In the thirteenth chapter of the book of Revelation, it is said that **every single person on Earth will actually *worship* the antichrist — except those who are true Christians.** Are we moving toward a world religion in our day?

One example that suggests this may the case was the convening of the Parliament of World Religions in the summer of 1993. Over 150 religions from Buddhism to Catholicism were represented at this meeting. The outcome of the meeting was **"The Declaration of a *Global Ethic*" which sought to outline the core values and beliefs common to all faiths.** Then in the fall of 1994, over 200 spiritual leaders met in Khartoum, Sudan to discuss the need for a world council of religions which would represent all faiths. Such a council would foster cooperation between the world's major religions. Those who attended not only **called for peace and religious harmony between the world's religions**, but they called for a _new political order_ as well. As a Buddhist Monk put it, "the unity of religion promoted by the Holy Father Pope John Paul II and approved by his holiness the Dalai Lama is not a goal to be achieved immediately, but a day may come when the love and compassion which both Buddha and Christ preached so eloquently will unite the world in a common effort to save humanity from senseless destruction, **by leading it toward the light in which we all believe**."[57]

235 *A World-Wide Shopping Mall*

The third core part of this new world order is a global economy. The Apostle John said in the 13th chapter of the book of Revelation that this new international economic order would dominate everyone on Earth. But, a truly global economy was not possible until today. Before the advent of modern communication and transportation systems, the world was little more than a collection of economic islands. However, there is no denying the fact that the same generation that saw Israel come back in her land, is also seeing the world's economic focus set clearly on free trade zones, the reduction of tariffs and the building of "the new global economy"! As US President Bill Clinton puts it, **"this new global economy is here to stay. We can't wish it away. We can't run from it. We can't build walls around our nation. So we must provide world leadership, we must compete, not retreat."**[58]

236 *Global State Troopers*

The Apostle John, foresaw that the rules of this new world order would be enforced by **a global army that will become so powerful that people will ask "who can make war"**[59] **with it?** Once again, there has never been anything resembling a world army since the times of the Romans — and that certainly wasn't an army that represented the whole world. But today, multinational military operations have become the norm — in places like Somalia, Iraq, and Bosnia, just to mention a few. Moreover, with the collapse of the Soviet Union, the role of NATO is currently being re-defined and reshaped into a kind of "global cop". As NATO Supreme Allied Commander Atlantic General John J. Sheen said of one recent exercise, "It is through exercises such as this that truly **we can create a new world order in which the militaries of the world can work in coordination and cooperation."**[60] We don't know what form this global cop will ultimately take on, but once again, you would have to agree that this is clearly something that is being given serious attention by our world leaders today. Just as the prophets said it would be.

237 *The Empire Strikes Back!*

One of the most remarkable prophecies in the Bible is found in the ninth chapter of the book of the prophet Daniel. Writing 500 years before the time of Christ, he peered into the future and saw that Jerusalem and her beloved temple would be destroyed. Historically, we know that this happened in 70 AD when the Roman armies under Titus flattened the city and the Second Temple. But, Daniel also foresaw something else. He said that the people who did this would be the people from whom the last days antichrist would arise. Speaking of this coming prince' he said, "the people of the prince that shall come shall destroy the city and the sanctuary..."[61] But, the Roman Empire has been dead for over 1,500 years. If this prophecy were to be fulfilled, the Roman Empire would have to arise once again onto the world scene.

Consider this. In 1951 the European Coal and Steel Community [ECSC] came into being. Later, in 1957, with the signing of the **Treaty of Rome**, the ECSC was altered again and became the European Economic Community. As time went by, the EEC extended its reach beyond economics and became the European Community. However, by the mid 1990's, being a described as a community no longer seemed appropriate, and so it became the European Union. Today that Union which makes up the largest free trade zone in the world, is about to have its own European currency. And it has already begun to form an army. Moreover, **it is no secret that the EU is made up of much the same territory that once belonged to the Holy Roman Empire.**

Former German Chancellor Helmut Kohl saw this emerging empire in Biblical terms. He proclaimed that "The United States of Europe will form the core of a peaceful order...the age prophesied of old, when all shall dwell secure and none shall make them afraid."[62] However the Russian communist, Leon Trotsky, writing in 1917 saw it more in this-worldly terms: **"the task of the proletariat is to create a United States of Europe, as a foundation for the United States of the World."**

238 *The Kings of the East!*

The 9th chapter of the book of Revelation contains a remarkable prophecy. Here the Apostle John, looking foward into the last days, saw an army coming from the east of the Euphrates River to attack Israel. What is particularily interesting is the fact that John saw the size of the army. He said, "And the number of the army...was two hundred thousand thousand."[63]. Considering the size of the known world population in John's day, that is an unthinkable number. In fact, it was not until modern times, with the population explosion in China and India, that such an idea was even possible. Today, China and India alone comprise 40% of the world population! With 2 billion citizens, an army of 200 million is not all that hard to imagine.

Peace in Our Time?

Despite the very real tensions in our world today, there is optimism. Now that the Cold War is over, the world seems to believe that we can build a safe and prosperous new world order. While the US and the former Soviet Union have now begun to sign treaties for the dismantling of weapons and the reduction of troops, it seems that the prophets had already foreseen this shift in attitude. The Apostle Paul said that in the last days the cry of the world would be one of **peace and safety**.[64] Today, peace seems to be breaking out almost everywhere. Israel has signed a peace treaty with Jordan and Egypt and is also progressively working out a peace process with the Palestinians. The world community worked very hard to bring peace to the former Yugoslavia, and on March 21, 1995 fifty-two European nations, the United States and Canada signed "The Stability Pact" known also as the Balladur Plan. Attached to the pact are about ninety-two "good neighborliness and cooperation agreements and arrangements." Also, **in the spring of 1994, the US federal government announced that it was scrapping its eleven year old "Doomsday Project."** The program provided underground bunkers for key US officials and outlined an unbreakable chain of command for military and civilian leaders in the case of a nuclear attack. The world, it seems, is indeed beginning to say "peace and safety."

There is a second part to the above noted prophecy, however. In his first letter to the Thessalonians the Apostle Paul says that *after* people start saying peace and safety, "then sudden destruction cometh upon them."[65] Likewise, Daniel says that the antichrist will come promising peace but "by peace shall destroy many."[66] The world situation today seems remarkably similar to the scenario laid out by the prophets — a world that says 'peace and safety' but that has real reason to be concerned. While many nations of the world signed the Nuclear Non-Proliferation Treaty, others refused to put their signatures on it as long as nations like Israel, India and Pakistan, which are all believed to possess nuclear capabilities, have not signed it. Other nations refused to sign while nuclear capabilities remain in the hands of the five super powers. Many are agreed that the world need not fear a nuclear holocaust as long as common sense prevails. However, the world, when dealing with pariah nations and terrorists, is not always dealing with common sense. Reports came out in 1995 from defectors from Saddam Hussein's family that there was a great deal of research and weaponry for **chemical and germ warfare** in Iraq that had not been uncovered by UN inspectors after the Gulf war. **There is also great fear that the former Soviet Union has not done a very good job of keeping track of its nuclear weapons or the materials needed to create those weapons.** Several cases of smuggled nuclear weapons materials making their way into Europe have already been uncovered and we can only begin to speculate about how much of this material is already in the hands of terrorists. Today, the possibility of sudden destruction coming in the midst of cries of peace is far from remote!

241 *The United Nations has it Backwards*

The cornerstone on the United Nations headquarters in New York City contains the verse from the book of Isaiah that promises that men shall "beat their swords into plowshares."[67] However, that prophecy is speaking about the time when the Messiah is ruling over His kingdom after He returns to this Earth. Man's attempt at building his own new world order ends in exactly the opposite way according to the prophet Joel who says, "Beat your plowshares into swords, and your pruninghooks into spears: let the weak say I am strong."[68] The phrase "let the weak say I am strong" puzzled Bible interpreters for years. In past generations nations were either weak or strong, but today, any nation, however weak, can become strong simply by adding nuclear weapons to its arsenals.

242 *The Mother of all Rumors*

When Jesus was asked about the last generation, one of the descriptions that He gave is that there would be "wars and rumors of wars."[69] The phrase rumors of wars' is an interesting one for this generation. No other generation has had the nuclear Sword of Damocles hanging over it the way we have. And the fact is that the rumor' of potential thermo-nuclear war did lead to the birth of the largest social movement in history — the peace movement.

243 — The Democratic Kingdom of Antichrist

The Prophet Daniel, in describing the empire that would rule the world in the last days, said the kingdom would be made "partly of iron and partly of clay."[70] The iron of a country can be seen in its military — for example, the *Iron Curtain* or the *Iron Fist* of Rome. But, the reference to clay is also interesting. Throughout the Bible clay is a symbol of man[71]. Thus a kingdom of clay has long been interpreted by Bible students as a "Kingdom of the People." Today, a world which feared communism sweeping westward is finding that instead, democracy (of the people, by the people, for the people') is sweeping eastward. As the two systems adapt to embrace each other, as is the case in Eastern Europe, we may be beginning to see the formative stages of one empire made "partly of iron and partly of clay."

244 — My Tribe Can Beat Up Your Tribe

Following the end of WWII in 1945, the allied nations divided the world up. But instead of finding peace, the world found itself in the midst of the Cold War, symbolized by the Russian construction of the Berlin Wall. The communist rulers of the day squelched tribal hostilities beneath their iron fist for decades. But, with the end of the Cold War, these tribal tensions began to surface once again. The war in the former Yugoslavia is a perfect example. There are also ethnic tensions in other former Soviet nations like Azerbaijan and Khazakstan. At the same time, there are tribal tensions in African nations like Burundi and Rwanda where the Hutus are fighting with the Tutsis. Even peaceful nations are experiencing some forms of ethnic tension. Take Canada, for example, where French Canadians in Quebec almost chose to leave the country. In the United Sates, racial strife threatens to turn major cities into battlegrounds. Reaction to the Rodney King verdict shows just how far the polarization has gone. In reality though, it does feel like the world is moving in the direction of peace, but there are major conflicts and tensions that center largely around ethic differences. And, this rise in the tensions between tribes, clans, or races was predicted in the Bible. **Jesus said in Matthew 24:7 that "nation will rise against nation", but the Greek word He used for nation was** *ethnos*, **meaning tribe or ethnic group.**

245   *Mystery Babylon*

In the 17th chapter of the book of Revelation, the Apostle John describes the united world religion of the last days as a religious "whore" who has the name "Mystery Babylon" written on her. The religion of the ancient Babylonians was very heavily influenced by astrology, magic, fortune-telling and occultism. In recent years our modern world has seen a remarkable increase in interest in the same types of ideologies that made up the Babylonian culture. Businessmen and politicians are having their astrological charts drawn up. Political leaders in Russia and Saudi Arabia are reported to use black magic, or to consult soothsayers for their political ends. Police authorities even use psychics to provide them with clues and tips in criminal cases. In fact, it was reported in late 1995 that **the CIA had been using six different psychics over a period of 20 years for intelligence missions**. **A recent nationwide poll sponsored by the University of Chicago found that 67% of Americans now claim to have had psychic experiences.** As one researcher noted: "While skeptical observers over the past twenty years have persisted in labeling it a 'fad' and predicting its imminent passing, the New Age Movement has quietly but relentlessly gathered momentum. Viewing this unprecedented phenomena with considerable hope, **some researchers have called it the most powerful force for positive change in human history.**"

246   *AIDS and The Bible*

It wasn't too long ago that scientists thought they were finally getting the upper hand on disease. With the increasing use of antibiotics it seemed that widespread disease — or pestilence as the Bible calls it — was on its way to becoming a thing of the past. But that is no longer the case. Diseases like tuberculosis, once thought to have been totally eradicated, are now resurfacing. Other strange new diseases are also appearing. There's streptococcus A, the flesh-eating virus, and there was also the Ebola outbreak in Zaire. Doctors are now finding themselves losing the battle as microbes are becoming immune to all the antibiotics that we have. AIDs is just one example of the new 'smart virus.' Even the bacteria that causes pneumonia is evolving into forms that cannot be treated by modern medicine. **World travel, changing sexual habits, and increasing numbers of refugees have made it possible for many of these diseases to become pandemic, rapidly spreading across the entire planet almost overnight.** At a microbiology conference in Sydney, Australia in July 1992 Frank Fenner of Canberra's John Curtin School of Medical Research warned that a pandemic plague actually seems inevitable! When Jesus was asked what the days just before his coming would be like, the sixth characteristic He gave was that of pestilence — worldwide disease.[72] In past generations, before the advent of world travel, this was simply not possible. Instead diseases could be limited by geography. Today deadly diseases can travel the globe just as easily as infected people can.

247 *World Wide Food Crisis*

The fifth characteristic that Jesus mentioned when asked about the last days was the spread of major famines.[73] In 1991 and 1992, Southern Africa suffered from a major drought, and later, in mid-1995, the continent suffered from a poor harvest, only about 40% of what had been harvested the year before. Botswana, with a crop failure of about 90%, had to declare a state of emergency and more than 10 million people were expected to face hunger as a result of the poor harvests of 1995. **Most people have come to believe that famine can only strike the desert climates of African nations, but clearly this is no longer the case.** Russia, in recent years, has been facing a famine of its own. And more recently, oil spills caused by old, decayed pipelines are ruining the rivers that supply water for humans, reindeer and cattle. The oil spills have also been destroying fish stocks and the poultry industry has dropped drastically. Official estimates suggested a 50% increase in the cost of bread for 1996. Ukraine is facing the same problems while intelligence sources have also suggested that China would probably face grain shortages too, after facing a serious drought in 1995. Reports in late 1995 warned that grain stocks were at an all time low after a drought in Australia. **Most experts now agree that one major natural disaster, or weather catastrophe, could mean a major food crisis that would be felt worldwide.**

248 *I'm All Shook Up*

The seventh thing that Jesus said when describing the world in the moments before His return, was the fact that we would see an increase in earthquakes.[74] Well, according to sources from Energy, Mines and Resources Canada there were, from 1900 to 1969, about 48 earthquakes that registered at 6.5 or more on the Richter Scale. This is an average of **6 per decade**. From 1970 to 1989 there were 33 earthquakes measuring 6.5 or more. This is an average of **17 per decade**. From January 1990 to July 1990 there were 10 earthquakes of 6.5 or greater. This is 10 major earthquakes in just six months. And from July 1990 to October 1992 there were 133 earthquakes which measured at 6.5 or greater. This averages out to **600 per decade**. In 1995 we saw major earthquakes in Japan, Manzanillo, Mexico and Russia. Residents of California and Vancouver, Canada have been warned that the "Big One" is coming. Roger Bilham, a geologist at the University of Colorado warned his audience at a gathering of the International Union of

Geodesy and Geophysics that super cities with a population of 2 million or more have been built up along major fault lines. His warning to the audience was nothing less than chilling: **"It's virtually certain there will be catastrophes in the coming decades, the likes of which we have never seen."**[75]

249 *The Ozone Hole*

Ozone is a gas (O_3) that makes up the ozonosphere which is about 6 to 30 miles above the Earth's surface. It protects the Earth from the sun's harmful ultraviolet rays. Already, this protective layer allows enough ultraviolet rays to get through to cause sunburns, and in some cases skin cancer. But **in recent years there has been an alarming increase in the number of cases of skin cancer and many of these cases are being blamed on the depletion of the ozone layer.** On top of that, it was discovered not too long ago that there was an ozone "hole" over Antarctica. By the mid 1990's the hole in the ozone layer was larger than Europe! The Bible may well have foretold this event in the 16th chapter of the book of Revelation. The Apostle John, peering into our day, said, "And the fourth angel poured out his vial upon the sun; and power was given unto him to scorch men with fire....And (they) blasphemed the God of heaven because of their pains and their sores..."[76]

250 *How about that Weather*

Hundred year storms are storms so powerful that they happen only once every hundred years or

so. By one count there have been four such storms
in the last five years. Here in North America, our
thoughts go to Hurricane Andrew, or the flooding of
the Mississippi Valley. But such phenomena stretch
well beyond North America. A recent report was
created by 1,580 scientists from over 69 nations.
Titled **"World Scientists Warning to Humanity"**,
it concluded that "Human beings and the
natural world are on a collision course." Even
Time Magazine in reporting on hurricanes, tornadoes
and monsoon's refer to "weird weather phenomena."
Jesus, in describing the last days, said to watch for
"the sea and the waves roaring."[77]

251 *Morality Caught With Pants Down*

In speaking of the last days, the Bible said
that "iniquity," or wickedness, "shall abound."[78] One
of the best ways to know what a society is all about,
is through its culture. Today because of tell-a-vision
the first global culture is emerging. And it is no
secret that the world is being inundated with violent
and sexually promiscuous programs which open the
world up to the most deviant ideas. Likewise,
contemporary rock music is, for the most part,
preoccupied with sex, drugs, or the occult. And the
arts? Well, there was Andres Serrano's "Piss
Christ" which was **a crucifix soaking in a jar of**
urine. In 1994 a sculpture was put on display in front
of the City Hall in Kansas City. The sculpture was of
eight, 4-foot tall stick men who were sexually
aroused. When city officials covered the genitalia on
the statues with garbage bags the Civil Liberties
Union filed a lawsuit. Then there was the display of

"The Dinner Party," featuring **depiction's of women's genitalia on dinner plates,** at the University of the District of Columbia. Roberta Cohen's "Confronting Your Fears" depicts **a male figure with an erection strangling a female figure.** While such "art" does not reflect the morals of all individuals in society, it is becoming more prevalent, and those who oppose it, like believers in Biblical Christianity, are being portrayed as censoring bigots, and are being told by the courts to simply put up and shut up'.

252 *Violence*

Jesus said that the last days would be like the days of Noah.[79] The Bible records the charactistics of those days. Genesis 6:11 says "...and the Earth was filled with violence." Today, no one can watch the evening news and not know that we live in a far more violent world than has ever existed in the past. While the world has known plenty of war, the 'everyday' violence in the world is on a dramatic increase. In fact, according to the FBI's own statistics there has been a 560% increase in violent crime in the United States since 1960. In the former Soviet Union things are much worse. Boris Yelsin has even considered putting army troops into the streets to serve as anti-crime patrols.

253 *Homosexuality on the Rise*

Today, all over the globe, in nation after nation, laws and charters are being altered to protect the rights of homosexuals and lesbians. People are being told that we should accept these "alternative" lifestyles. Christians who preach otherwise are condemned as religious, narrow-minded bigots. Education curriculum on homosexuality and lesbianism have been slipped into many health care and sex education programs in the public school system. **Reading materials like "Daddy's Roommate" and "Heather Has Two Mommies" are becoming a common part of school curriculum.** US presidents George Bush and Bill Clinton have invited homosexual and lesbian lobby groups to the White House, giving them recognition as just another special interest movement. Jesus did say that the end times would be "as it was in the days of Lot."[80] The days of Lot, of course, were famous for the destruction of Sodom and Gomorrah where homosexuality was rampant.

254 *Longing for Opie Taylor*

The Apostle Paul gave a piercing description of the last generation: "For men shall be lovers of them own selves, covetous, boasters, proud, blasphemers, disobedient to parents, unthankful, unholy, without natural affection, trucebrakers, false accusers, incontinent, fierce, despisers of those that are good, traitors, heady, highminded, lovers of pleasures more than lovers of God..." No one can any longer argue that ours is just another generation of young people exercising a new fad. Many schools in the US have had to resort to installing weapon detectors at the front door. And, that's no random decision. **Those monitoring the situation warn that the trend in teen violence is an epidemic.** One of the latest such trends is children killing their own parents. Perhaps the most famous case is that of the Menendez brothers. But there are numerous similar cases. 15-year-old Jason Edward Lewis killed his parents because he was angry about a midnight curfew.[81] A seventeen year old honor student had been charged for bringing a gun to school. He was sentenced to do community service by the courts. His parents further punished him by taking away the keys to his truck and wouldn't allow him to listen to his favorite music. So he shot them along with his two sisters. Of course, most kids would never even contemplate such things. But, there is no other generation in human history that has had such widespread examples of the complete breakdown of society as we have today!

255 *The Sorcerer's New Apprentice*

The Apostle John tells us that in the last days one of the key attributes of society will be the widespread use of "sorceries." The Greek word for "sorceries" in this Bible reference is *pharmakeia,* from which we get our English words pharmacy and pharmaceuticals. So the reference to magic in this case is clearly related to drugs. There is no doubt that the Western world has a problem with drug use among its teenagers, and even among its younger children. But there is more than just a curious interest in drugs like marijuana and cocaine in today's world. Instead we are seeing a growing interest in mind-altering drugs and hallucinogenics like LSD. We are also seeing many up-scale professionals from North America and Europe flocking to areas of the Amazon because of a growing interest in shamanism. They want to study, through first-hand experience, just as Carlos Castaneda did with Native

Indian don Juan, the effects of psychedelic plants. Carlos Castaneda wrote a series of books on his experiments with mind-altering substances like peyote, and of his apprenticeship into shamanism. South American shamans are now allowing tourists to be their apprentices, giving them mixtures from a dozen or so psychedelic plants like the woody vine known as *ayahuasca,* so that they can learn to become mystically "at one" with the universe.

256   *The Serpent Speaks Again*

If you ever went to Sunday School, you will remember that the serpent enticed Eve to eat the forbidden fruit with the Lie.' **He told her that if she ate this fruit her eyes would be opened. She would become as a god and she would never die.**[82] This same lie, which has been at the heart of the eastern religions for thousands of years, has today been repackaged for the west and, just like Eve, millions of people are eating it up. **Maitreya**, who new age leader Benjamin Creme claims to be the 'christ', claims "man is an emerging God...My plan and my duty is to reveal to you a new way...which will permit the divine in man to shine forth." **Maharishi Mahesh Yogi**, the founder of Transcendental Meditation says "be still and know that you are god." Actress **Shirley Maclaine** tells millions through her books and media appearances that "you are everything....Maybe the tragedy of the human race was that we have forgotten that we are each divine....You must never worship anyone other than self. For you are God." There is no doubt that the serpent's lie is sweeping the world today. Further, **The Apostle Paul**, writing two thousand years ago, said that in the last days a strong delusion would come upon the Earth leading mankind to embrace this very lie![83]

257 *The Almighty Ego*

Almost in parallel to the re-emergence of the serpent's lie, is the Apostle Paul's prophecy that "in the last days perilous times shall come. For men shall be lovers of their own selves."[84] Today, in addition to the millions who now literally believe that they are gods, are the millions who have embraced the **human potential movement.** Driven by self-help seminars, training programs and best-selling books, these people are being taught the exact principles of eastern religions. Reporting on the run-away trend, the New York Times said that "Representatives of some of the nation's largest corporations, including **IBM, AT&T and General Motors,** met in New Mexico this summer to discuss **how metaphysics, the occult and Hindu mysticism might help executives compete in the marketplace."[85]** At the same time self-esteem classes have become the norm in public schools. The students of today are told that the way to success is through self-love, and that societies' problems are caused by a lack of self esteem.

258 *False Messiahs*

The very first thing that Jesus said about the last days was that there would be great deception and that "many shall come in my name, saying, I am Christ; and shall deceive many."[86] You may remember the horrific mass suicide of **Jim Jones'** followers several years ago. Then there's the Rev. Sun Myung Moon of the Unification Church who claims to be a messiah. Recently Rabbi **Menachem Schneerson** died in New York City. His Jewish followers, forming the Lubavitcher Movement, believed he was the messiah. In more recent days, **David Koresh**, another self-proclaimed messiah captivated media attention because of a fire that destroyed him and his followers at the Branch Davidian compound in Waco, Texas. At about the same time there was another catastrophic mass suicide/murder event in Switzerland. In that case, people had followed the teachings of **Luc Jouret** of the Order of the Solar Temple. Jouret also claimed that he was the Christ. For several years now Benjamin Creme has been claiming that **Maitreya**, a new age Christ, will reveal himself to the world soon. And the list goes on and on. But perhaps the greatest fulfillment of this prophecy is not found in the cases of these deluded leaders. Instead, we need to recognize that **millions of new agers now walk around believing that they are gods.** Today, it seems that through the new age movement any Tom, Dick or Harry can be his own messiah!

259 *Signs and Wonders*

After He warned the disciples about false Christs and false prophets, Jesus warned them that these imposters would be capable of performing signs and wonders that would deceive people in a powerful way.[87] People from all around the world flock to Fatima and Medugorje hoping to see a vision of the virgin Mary. Gurus from the East, like Sai Baba, who can perform miraculous displays, attract hundreds of followers from the West. And, thousands of people are claiming to have been contacted by extra-terrestrials. A Roper poll in 1993 found that **18% of American adults claimed to have been woken up by aliens**, only to find themselves paralyzed. 2% of American adults actually claimed to have been abducted by these aliens! Thousands are flocking to trance-channelers, and sprit guides, in search for a supernatural experience….and many are finding it. As leading authors Whitley Strieber and Shirley MacLaine note, what has happened to them is happening to millions. **The signs and wonders they have witnessed have convinced them that they are real. What a perfect scenario for massive spiritual deception!**

260 *Doctrines of Devils*

The Apostle Paul and the Apostle Peter both warned that "seducing spirits" and "doctrines of devils"[88] would be prevalent in the last days. Today, **countless thousands of people around the world are ready and willing to seek the advice of spirits from another time and place.** People, including famous people like actresses **Shirley MacLaine** and **Linda Evans**, spend thousands of dollars at a time to listen to spirit entities speak through so-called trance channelers like **J.Z. Knight** or **Kevin Ryerson**. Pagan religions and native spirituality are resurfacing in a big way and everyday people are looking to shamans and witch-doctors for spiritual enlightenment. People even seek spirit guides in sessions with their physicians or psychologists, hoping these guides will show them the way to physical or mental well-being. Others claim to be getting messages from ET's and beings in between incarnations. Because of the remarkable fact that all of these messages — whether they supposedly come from ETs, spirit guides, angels, or channeled entities — all seem to be the same, people believe they are receiving truth and wisdom from beyond. **Indeed, the messages are very similar to each other** *and* **to the lie the serpent told to Eve in the Garden of Eden.** As one enthusiastic report pointed out, "Whatever the method of channeling, it is the content that is the most important, and here there is remarkable agreement, even unanimity, among the various channeled entities."

261   *'Blue' Genes*

So great will be the last days deception that even many who claim to be Christians are going to "depart from the faith."[89] In his second letter to the Thessalonians, the Apostle Paul said that before Christ comes again there is going to be apostasy, a falling away from the faith, in the churches that claim to represent Him.[90] A survey was recently done among **7,441 Protestant pastors**. The results were staggering. **Asked if they believed that the Bible is the inspired, inerrant Word of God: 87% of Methodists said NO. 95% of Episcopalians said NO. 82% of Presbyterians said NO. 67% of American Baptists said NO.** And, the list goes on and on. The examples of this departure are too numerous to mention. More and more, mainstream churches, which claim to represent Christ and the Word of God, are looking into the ordination of homosexuals, despite the fact that the Bible condemns homosexuality as sin.

Bishop Holloway, the **Anglican Bishop of Edinburgh, has claimed that God-given genes cause us to commit adultery**. Yet the Bible condemns adultery as sin. The Church of England's board of social responsibility put out a report titled "Something to Celebrate" which looked at the possibility of condoning co-habitation without marriage. Yet the Bible condemns fornication. Surely we are witnessing the apostasy of the last days, just as the Bible told us we would.

262 *It's Those Crazy Christians Again*

The Bible tells us that during the last days, people are going to mock those who believe in the second coming of Jesus Christ. The Apostle Peter calls these people "scoffers" who would ask "Where is the promise of His coming?"[91] Surprisingly, some of the leading examples of this phenomenon are church leaders! For example, Rev. David Ebaugh, says, "You can study a book about going to heaven in a so-called rapture if that turns you on. We want to study the Bible to learn to live and love and to bring heaven to Earth." Likewise, the former Archbishop of Canterbury, Sir Robert Runcie believes that all religions should try to come together into a great ecumenical religion. The only ones not welcome are those who look for the Second Coming. According to Runcie, "...nor can we accept the despair of those who interpret the various crises we face today...as harbingers of the end of the world. The fatalism inherent in such a philosophy has no part in authentic religious awareness." In 1994 Charles B. Strozier wrote a book titled *On The Psychology of*

Fundamentalism. In that book, he noted that the fastest-growing part of Christianity was apocalyptic and millennial, hoping for the return of Christ at the end of the Battle of Armageddon. Strozier tries to explain the movement through psychoanalysis. He claims that those who adhere to the movement are "unsteady" and dangerous. They suffer, he says, from **"a kind of collective illness."**

263 *Hatred of Christians Foretold*

Jesus told his disciples that in the end times, Christians would be hated for His name's sake.[92] The name "Christian" has become as much of a "byword" to the world in recent years as the name "Jew". Part of the reason for this is that the world is moving far away from the Christian values that used to guide such a large portion of it. Today the outright attack has begun. Star Trek creator Gene Roddenberry summed the anti-God view. Writing in Time Magazine he said, "if the future is not for the fainthearted, it is even more certainly not for the cowardly...**Those who insist that theirs is the only correct government or economic system deserve the same contempt as those who insist they have the only true God."** Today, through the power of television, a world is being fed an anti-Christian agenda. It has been so successful that a recent poll showed that Americans would least like to live next door to a cult member. Number two was a fundamentalist!

264   *The Only Savior*

The Bible is the only book that contains such a vast collection of prophecies relating to the nation of Israel, other nations in the world, specific cities, and the entire human race. **And it is the only Book that contains prophecies about a Savior for the human race — the Messiah**. As Wilbur Smith noted, "Mohammedanism cannot point to any prophecies of the coming of Mohammed uttered hundreds of years before his birth. Neither can the founders of any cult in this country rightly identify any ancient text specifically foretelling their appearance."[93]

265   *Plenty of Notice*

The Old Testament includes about sixty different prophecies, with more than 300 references, of the coming of the Messiah. It was through the fulfillment of these prophecies that Israel was told she would be able to recognize the true Messiah when He came. The four gospels record several times when Jesus said that He was fulfilling a prophecy of the Old Testament. Luke 24:27 records, for example, "And beginning at Moses and all the prophets, he expounded unto them in all the scriptures the things concerning himself." And verse 44 notes, "And he said unto them, These are the words which I spake unto you, while I was yet with you, that all things must be fulfilled, which were written in the law of Moses, and the prophets and the psalms, concerning me."

266 *Natural' Childbirth*

Genesis 3:15 gives the first prophecy of the coming of the Messiah. In this verse, we are told that He would come from "the seed of the woman." Galatians 4:4 tells us that Jesus Christ fulfilled this prophecy: "But when the fullness of the time was come, God sent forth his Son, made of a woman, made under the law."

267 *Born of a Virgin*

Isaiah 7:14 tells us that the "woman" would be a virgin. Matthew, chapter 1, and Luke, chapter 1, confirm this prophecy and tell us very clearly that Jesus Christ the Messiah was born of a virgin.

268 *The Son of God*

Psalm 2:7 says the Messiah would be the "Son of God." After Jesus was baptized and the dove descended on Him, God said, "This is My beloved Son, in whom I am well-pleased" (Matthew 3:17).

269 *That's Pretty Specific*

Psalm 110:4 said that the Messiah would be a priest from the order of Melchisedec. Hebrews 5:6 says, "Thou art a priest for ever after the order of Melchisedec."

270   *The Seed of Abraham*

God promised His faithful servant Abraham that the Messiah would be his descendant (Genesis 22:18). The genealogy given in Matthew 1 confirms that Jesus Christ was indeed a descendent from the seed of Abraham.

271   *Family Tree Prophesied*

Jeremiah 23:5 and Psalm 89:3-4 tell us that the Messiah would come from the lineage of King David. The gospels of Matthew and Luke give the Messiah's genealogy, again proving the fulfillment of this prophecy. At first it appears that the two genealogies of Matthew and Luke do not agree. However, the lineage in Matthew is of Joseph while Luke's genealogy is of Mary. **It is through Mary's genealogy (the "seed" of the woman, since Joseph was not the biological father of Jesus), that Jesus' family tree could be traced back to King David.** Interestingly, Jesus' genealogical records were destroyed with the Jewish temple in 70 AD, making it impossible for any would-be Messiah after that date to prove that he was fulfilling this prophecy.

272   *John the Baptist, Foretold*

Malachi 3:1 tells us that a messenger would be sent before the coming of the Messiah to proclaim His coming. This prophecy was later fulfilled, and the messenger was John the Baptist (Matthew 3:3, 11:10; John 1:23; Luke 1:17).

273 *Birth and Taxes*

Micah 5:2 tells us that the Messiah would come out of the town of Bethlehem. Under the orders of Caesar Augustus' decree, mentioned in the gospel of Luke, chapter 2, everyone in the land was forced to return to their place of origin in order to pay their taxes. Because of this decree, Joseph and Mary had to return to Bethlehem where Jesus Christ was born, thus fulfilling Micah's prophecy.

274 *Healing Miracles*

Isaiah 35:5-6 teaches that the Messiah would perform many miracles. "Then the eyes of the blind shall be opened, and the ears of the deaf shall be unstopped. Then shall the lame man leap as an hart, and the tongue of the dumb sing." The four gospels give many accounts of such miracles performed by Jesus Christ.

275 *Parables*

Psalm 78:2 said the Messiah would speak in parables and the four gospels do make several references to the parables that Jesus used in His teachings. Matthew 13:34, for example, says, **"All these things spake Jesus unto the multitude in parables, and without a parable spake he not unto them."**

276

Temple Needed to Fulfill Prophecy

The Messiah had to come while there was a Jewish Temple since the prophecy in Malachi 3:1 says He would "suddenly come to his temple..." Matthew 21:12 says that **Jesus entered "the temple of God, and cast out all them that sold and bought in the temple..."** This temple was destroyed completely in 70 AD by the Romans and there has not been another one since.

277

Right On Time

The Bible also prophesied that the Messiah would have to come before Israel lost their right to judge their own people.[94] Israel lost that right in 11 AD when the Sanhedrin lost its right to pass the death sentence, according to the Jewish historian Josephus.[95] **Combined with the previous prophecy about the Temple we know that the Messiah had to come before 11 AD and no later than 70 AD. Jesus, fulfills both of these prophecies.**

278

Practice of Crucifixion Foretold

Because the Jews were no longer able to try their own capital cases, Jesus was not stoned to death, which was the Jewish custom. Instead, He was crucified, which was the Roman method of execution. This is a fulfillment of King David's description of the Messiah's death in Psalm 22. **He described the crucifixion in great detail —** including the phrase "they pierced my hands and my feet" — **10 centuries before the actual crucifixion of Jesus Christ took place, and 700 years before crucifixion was ever even heard of in Israel!**

279 *Rejection by the Jews*

The prophets foresaw that the Jews would reject their Messiah. King David said that "The stone which the builders refused is become the head stone of the corner."[96] The Apostle Peter notes the fulfillment of this prophecy: **"Unto you therefore which believe he is precious: but unto them which be disobedient, the stone which the builders disallowed, the same is made the head of the corner."[97]**

280 *Right Down to the Day!*

The precise timing of Jesus' crucifixion was also given to the Jews when God revealed to the prophet Daniel (9:24) how the Jews could calculate the day of the revealing of the Messiah. Talking of a 490 year period, the prophet foresaw that it would begin "from the going forth of the commandment to restore and build Jerusalem" (9:25). In the book of Nehemiah we learn that this command was given "in the month Nisan [on the Hebrew calendar], in the twentieth year of the king" (2:1). The king was Artaxerxes Longimanus who ruled from 465 to 425 BC. The date of this command has been calculated at Nisan 1, 445 BC. **The prophet Daniel said that**

483 years from that date, the Messiah would be revealed to Israel, but then He would then "be cut off but not for himself"(9:26). This prophecy refers to the crucifixion when Jesus died, or was cut off, for the sins of the world. **483 years later, to the day, was Sunday, April 6, 32 AD. On that day, which we commemorate as Palm Sunday, Jesus rode into Jerusalem on a donkey and revealed himself as Israel's Messiah.** He was killed four days later, thus fulfilling the prophecy that He would be revealed and then slain.

281 *Passover Prophecy*

The dates on which Jesus was taken by the Roman authorities and then slain also coincided precisely with the Jewish Passover. Jesus became the Passover Lamb, "without blemish". At the first Passover, described in Exodus 12, God instructed the Israelites to kill a lamb with no blemishes and to put its blood on their door posts. When the angel of death passed through Egypt where the Israelites were being held as slaves, it would pass by any house that had the blood of a Passover lamb on its door posts. Jesus fulfilled Moses' prophecy of the Passover Lamb because it is through His blood that we can be saved from, or passed over by, death.

282 *His Bones Must Be Unbroken*

In describing the Passover ritual, Exodus 12 says that no bones of the Passover lamb were to be broken. Psalm 34:20 prophesied that the bones of the

Messiah would not be broken. John 19:33 tells us that the Roman centurion, seeing that Jesus was already dead on the cross, did not break His legs, as was the custom, to speed up His death.

283   *Riding on a Donkey*

On the day in which Jesus rode into Jerusalem on a donkey, "the colt of an ass," He fulfilled a prophecy spoken by the prophet Zechariah 500 years earlier. Zechariah had said, **"Rejoice greatly, O daughter of Zion; shout, O daughter of Jerusalem; behold, thy King cometh unto thee: he is just, and having salvation; lowly, and riding upon an ass, and upon a colt the foal of an ass."[98]**

284   *The Greatest Miracle*

The Bible also foretold the resurrection. Psalm 16:10 prophesies that the Messiah would say, "For thou wilt not leave my soul in hell; neither wilt thou suffer thine Holy One to see corruption." The fulfillment was recorded in Acts 2:31: "He seeing this before spake of the resurrection of Christ, that his soul was not left in hell, neither his flesh did see corruption."

285   *The Ascension Foretold*

The prophecy of Christ's ascension into heaven after He was resurrected was also written in the 68th Psalm. The fulfillment was recorded in Acts 1:9: "And when he had spoken these things, while they beheld, he was taken up; and a cloud received him out of their sight."

286 — *The Right is Right*

Psalm 110:1 tells us that Christ would be seated at the right hand of God. Hebrews 1:3 says, "When he had by himself purged our sins, sat down on the right hand of the Majesty on high."

287 — *Messiah Pierced*

Zechariah 12:10 says that one day, when He comes again, the Jews will look on their Messiah "whom they pierced". First of all, His hands and feet were pierced with nails to the cross. Also, John 19:34 tells us that the Roman centurion pierced Jesus' side and blood and water came out.

288 — *Sold!*

The prophet Zechariah[99] said that the Messiah would be sold for thirty pieces of silver. The 27th chapter of Matthew reveals that Jesus had been betrayed by Judas Iscariot for exactly that amount.

289 — *Betrayed by a Friend*

Psalm 41:9 said that it would be a friend "which did eat my bread" that would betray the Messiah. Judas walked with Jesus and the disciples during His ministry on Earth, and he also ate the bread and wine that Jesus offered at the last supper in the upper room.

290 *Guilty Conscience*

Zechariah 11:13 said that the thirty pieces of silver for which the Messiah was sold would be thrown "in the house of the Lord." Matthew 27:5 tells us that when Judas realized what he had done, he threw down the thirty pieces of silver onto the temple floor and then killed himself.

291 *Potter's Lucky Day*

Zechariah 11:13 tells us exactly what this money would be used for after it was thrown on the floor of the temple. The prophet said the money would be thrown to the "potter." Matthew 27:7 records that the chief priests used these thirty pieces of silver to buy a potter's field to bury strangers in.

292 *The Defense Rests*

Isaiah 53:7 prophesied that the Messiah "opened not his mouth" to defend Himself against His accusers. Matthew 27:12 records: "And when he was accused of the chief priests and elders, he answered nothing."

293 *Beating Described*

The prophet Isaiah said Christ's accusers would spit in His face, they would strike His back and pluck out His beard.[100] Matthew 26:67 gives the fulfillment of this prophecy: "Then they did spit in his face, and buffeted him; and others smote him with palms of their hands."

294   *In the Company of Thieves*

Isaiah said He would be "numbered with the transgressors."[101] This prophecy was fulfilled clearly when Jesus was crucified along with two thieves.

295   *Hatred Without Cause*

Psalm 69:4 said the Messiah would be hated for no reason. The fulfillment of this prophecy was given in John 15:25: "But this cometh to pass, that the word might be fulfilled that is written in their law, They hated me without a cause."

296   *The Gamblers*

The fact that people would wager bets for Christ's garments at the crucifixion was also prophesied in the Old Testament.[102] The fulfillment is given in John 19:23-24 where we are told: "Then the soldiers, when they had crucified Jesus, took his garments, and made four parts, to every soldier a part; and also his coat: now the coat was without seam, woven from the top throughout. They said therefore among themselves, Let us not rend it, but cast lots for it, whose it shall be: that the scripture might be fulfilled which saith, They parted my raiment among them, and for my vesture they did cast lots. These things therefore the soldiers did."

297 *That Doesn't Help*

It was also prophesied that Jesus would be given vinegar and gall to drink when He was thirsty (Psalm 69:21). Matthew 27:34 says, "They gave him vinegar to drink mingled with gall; and when he had tasted thereof, he would not drink."

298 *Word For Word*

Christ's cry of being forsaken on the cross was prophesied in Psalm 22. Verse 1 said He would cry out, "why hast thou forsaken me? why art thou so far from helping me...?" Matthew 27:46 records: "And at the ninth hour Jesus cried with a loud voice, saying, Eli, Eli, lama sabachthani? that is to say, My God, my God, why hast thou forsaken me?"

299 *Luxury Accommodations*

Isaiah 53:9 said He would be buried as a rich man. The fulfillment of this prophecy was recorded in Matthew 27 where we are told that Jesus was buried in the tomb of Joseph of Arimathea, who was a rich man.

300 *Let's Be Realistic Here*

Many try to explain away the fulfillment of these prophecies by saying that Jesus knew about them beforehand and tried to make it look like He was fulfilling them all to trick

everyone. But how could He control being born in
Bethlehem? How could He control being born of the
lineage of David? How could He control being born
before the scepter passed from Judah, but during the
time of Roman rule so that He would die by
crucifixion, and before the temple was destroyed
along with His genealogical record? How could He
control when He would be crucified? How could He
control how much money Judas would betray Him
for? How could He be sure that the chief priests
would use this money to buy a potter's field? How
could He be sure that after He died, the Roman
centurion would not break His legs? How could He
be sure that the Roman centurion would pierce His
side with a spear? There are just too many
prophecies that have been filled with absolute
perfection by Jesus Christ for anyone to remain a
skeptic about His identity.

301 *That is Simply Impossible*

Josh McDowell, in his book *Evidence That
Demands a Verdict* gave an example of the
likelihood of even eight such prophecies coming true
by chance. "The following probabilities are taken
from Peter Stoner in *Science Speaks* to show that
by using the modern science of probability in
reference to eight prophecies... ...We find that the
chance that any man might have lived down to the
present time and fulfilled all eight prophecies is 1 in
10^{17}.' That would be 1 in 100,000,000,000,000,000. In
order to help us comprehend this staggering
probability, Stoner illustrates it by supposing that we
take 10^{17} silver dollars and lay them on the face of
Texas. They will cover all the state two feet deep.

Now mark one of these silver dollars and stir the whole mass thoroughly, all over the state. Blindfold a man and tell him that he can travel as far as he wishes, but he must pick up one silver dollar and say that this is the right one. What chance would he have of getting the right one? Just the same chance that the prophets would have had of writing these eight prophecies and having them all come true in any one man, from their day to the present time, providing they wrote them in their own wisdom."[103]

301 Startling Proofs & Prophecies

Proving That God Exists

In Conclusion

New age evolutionists suggest that man will continue to evolve, not physically, but into a higher spiritual and intellectual species. But how long does man have? Scientists have proven that the present universe is not eternal. It *is* wearing down and it *is* running out. Will that simply be the end then? While scientific evidence tells us this world will indeed end, does that mean that man is not an eternal being either? The Bible too tells us that the present heavens and Earth are going to pass away (II Peter 3:7). But the Bible also suggests that man is an eternal being. Therefore, we need to give serious thought to where we want to spend eternity.

We believe we have provided sufficient evidence to get even the most die-hard atheist or skeptic to at least think about his or her world view and about his or her purpose in life. The evidence demands that a verdict be reached. Does God exist? Does Jesus Christ exist? Is He the Messiah, the Savior of mankind through whom we can obtain eternal life in heaven? These are questions we hope you will think about seriously. The creationist view not only provides satisfactory answers for where we came from, but also, why we are here and where we are going.

Perhaps you were a die-hard atheist, or a strong skeptic. But now you believe that God does really exist. And you may now be willing to believe that everything God says in His word, the Bible, has come true just as He said, and will come true just as He prophesied. Jesus died for the sins of all mankind. The only thing you have to do is recognize that you are one of the sinners who needs to be saved from sins. And you need to ask Jesus to forgive you of your sins, to come into your life, and to give you eternal salvation just as He promised. It's as simple as that. If you are ready to accept this in your heart, you can say this simple prayer to God:
Dear Father in heaven, I realize that I am a sinner and worthy of the fires of hell. At this moment I confess my sins and ask You to forgive me for my rebellion against You and my refusal to accept the love of Christ. I accept the sacrifice that Your Son Jesus made for me on Calvary's cross. I believe that You raised Him from the dead. I confess with my mouth that Jesus is my Lord. Thank You for hearing this prayer and accepting me into the family of God because of the blood of Christ that covers my sins. And I know that from this moment on I am saved. Thank You, Lord. ■

Index

[1] Asimov, Isaac, "In the Game of Energy and Thermodynamics You Can't Even Break Even," *Journal of the Smithsonian Institute* (June, 1970), p. 6.

[2] Nigel Hawkes, "Hunt On For Dark Secret of Universe," *London Times*, April 25, 1992, p. 1.

[3] *International Herald Tribune*, "US Scientists Find a Holy Grail': Ripples at the Edge of the Universe," April 24, 1992, p. 1.

[4] Ibid.

[5] *Time*, cover story, by Michael D. Lemonick and J. Madeleine Nash, March 6, 1995, p. 37.

[6] Wald, George, "The Origin of Life", *Physics and Chemistry of Life*, 1955, p. 12.

[7] *Time*, March 6, 1995 op. cit., p. 40.

[8] Ibid.

[9] Vardiman, Larry, *The Age of the Earth's Atmosphere*, Institute for Creation Research, 1990.

[10] Austin, Steven A. and Humphreys, Russell D.; "The Sea's Missing Salt: A Dilemma for Evolutionists," *Proceedings of the Second International Conference on Creationism*, Vol. 2, 1991; pp. 17-33.

[11] Sir Francis Crick, Scientific American (February, 1991)

[12] Stephen Hawking, 'A Brief History of Time', p.127

[13] Ross, Hugh, Ph.D.; *The Creator and the Cosmos;* NavPress; Colorado Springs, CO; 1993; p. 133.

[14] Darwin, Charles; *On the Origin of Species*, Second Ed.; (London, John Murray, 1860); p. 168.

[15] As quoted in Carlson, Ron and Decker, Ed; *Fast Facts on False Teachings;* Harvest House Publishers; Eugene, OR; 1994; p. 55.

[16] —Dr. Colin Patterson, senior palaeontologist at the British Museum of Natural History, responding to a letter from a reader of his book, Evolution.

[17] *Time*; December 4, 1995; "When Life Exploded" by J. Madeleine Nash; p. 73.

[18] *Time*; December 18, 1995; "Are the Bible's Stories True?" by Michael D. Lemonick; p. 68.

[19] As cited in Geisler, Howe; op. cit.

[20] Lea, John W.; *The Greatest Book in the World*; Philadelphia: n.p., 1929: as cited in McDowell, Josh; *Evidence that Demands a Verdict*, Vol. 1; Here's Life Publishers, Inc., San Bernardino, CA, 1979.

[21] McDowell, Josh; Evidence That Demands a Verdict; Here's Life Publishers, Inc., San Bernardino, CA. 1979. p. 20; citing Ramm Bernard, Protestant Christian Evidences; Chicago; Moody Press; 1957.

[22] Albright, William F.; *Recent Discoveries in Bible Lands*; New York; Funk and Wagnalls; 1955.

[23] McDowell, Josh; op. cit.; p. 70.

[24] Ibid.

[25] Ezekiel 38:8
[26] Isaiah 12:11-12
[27] Ezekiel 38:8
[28] Matthew 24:32; Luke 21:31
[29] Deuteronomy 28:64
[30] Deuteronomy 28:37; 65-66
[31] Ezekiel 38:8
[32] Ezekiel 38:14
[33] Zechariah 12:2-3
[34] Zephaniah 3:9
[35] Matthew 24:2
[36] Daniel 11:39
[37] Ezekiel 38:6,15; 39:2 Amplified
[38] Ezekiel 38:13
[39] Ezekiel 38:3,5,6 -Amplified Version of the Bible
[40] Ezekiel 38:7
[41] Jeremiah 16:15
[42] Ezekiel 38:13
[43] Ezekiel 39:4
[44] Revelation 13:16-17
[45] Washington Times, October 13, 1993.
[46] *Wired;* September 1995; "A Chip for Every Child?" by Simson Garfinkel.
[47] *Popular Science;* July 1995; "Money" by Phil Patton; p. 74.
[48] Revelation 13:16-17
[49] *New York Times;* March 28, 1995; "Letters to the Editor Section."
[50] *Popular Science;* October 1994.
[51] Revelation 13:16-17
[52] Terry Galanoy, Charge it! (New York:Putnum Publishers 1980); emphasis added.
[53] Revelation 13:16-17
[54] Final Warning Video, This Week in Bible Prophecy, 1995.
[55] Ibid.
[56] *Amarillo Daily News;* August 22, 1995; "Robot may become humanoid"; p. 10A.
[57] Catholic World May/June 1989 p.140
[58] International Herald Tribune July 6, 1993.
[59] Revelation 13:4
[60] The New American Nov 13, 1995 p.16
[61] Daniel 9:26
[62] Associated Press, June 8, 1990
[63] Revelation 9:16
[64] I Thessalonians 5:1-3
[65] I Thessalonians 5:1-3
[66] Daniel 8:25
[67] Isaiah 2:4
[68] Joel 3:10
[69] Matthew 24:6
[70] Daniel 2:41-42

71 Isaiah 45:9; 64:8
72 Matthew 24:7
73 Matthew 24:7
74 Matthew 24: 7
75 Reuters, "Earthquakes threaten big cities with disaster, geologist warns", July 4, 1995.
76 Revelation 16:9,11
77 Luke 21:25
78 Matthew 24:12
79 Luke 17:26
80 Luke 17:28
81 *Boston Globe;* March 15, 1995; as cited in the *Blumenfeld Education Letter;* March 1995.
82 Genesis 3:4-5
83 II Thessalonians 2:11
84 II Timothy 3:2
85 Robert Lindsey, New York Times, September 29, 1986.
86 Matthew 24:5
87 Matthew 24:24
88 I Timothy 4:1; II Peter 2:1
89 I Timothy 4:1
90 II Thessalonians 2:3
91 II Peter 3:3
92 Matthew 24:9
93 Smith, Wilbur M.; *The Incomparable Book*; Minneapolis; Beacon Publications, 1961.
94 Genesis 49:10
95 *Antiquities*; Book 17, Chapter 13:1-5
96 Psalm 118:22
97 I Peter 2:7
98 Zechariah 9:9.
99 Zechariah 11:12-13
100 Isaiah 50:6
101 Isaiah 53:12
102 Psalm 22:18
103 McDowell; op. cit.; p. 167.

The
following

This Week In
Bible Prophecy

*ministry
tools are
designed to
encourage
believers,
&
challenge
skeptics...*

This Week In Bible Prophecy
P.O. Box 665, Niagara Falls, Ontario L2E 6V5